The
GOD
equation

THE GOD EQUATION
Discover the Master's Degree in Science

ISBN: 978-0-924748-90-5
UPC: 88571300060-4

Printed in the United States of America
© 2008 by Bobby Lynn

Milestones International Publishers
140 Danika Drive NW
Huntsville, AL 35806
(256) 830-0362; Fax (256) 830-9206
www.milestonesintl.com

Cover design by: Thirty Thumbs Design Works

1 2 3 4 5 6 7 8 9 10 11 / 09 08 07 06 05 04

The
GOD
equation

Discover the Master's
Degree in Science

Bobby Lynn

MileStones
INTERNATIONAL PUBLISHERS

Table of Contents

Dedication

To all those who have pushed me beyond the limits I placed on myself, thank you. To The Rock Family Worship Center and my pastors, Rusty and Leisa Nelson, God bless you for all that you do for His Kingdom. We love you. To our associate pastors, Mark and Michelle Benson, thank you for your encouragement. The Dill family, the Krafts, and the Garrison bunch down on the compound, thank you for being who you are in God. We've learned so much from so many people that there isn't room to mention everyone.

To David Van Koevering for popping the quiff in my life and causing this book to be. You are an awesome man of God.

The anointed music of Jason Upton, JoAnn McFatter, Ray Hughes, and Suzy Yaraei played almost nonstop in my office while I wrote. Your music opens the heavens and revelation pours forth.

To my loving family: Tammy, my beautiful wife, I love you most! Tyler, my drummer boy, and Madison, my ballerina, may you only see your True Father in heaven through my love. He is the only thing in life worth pursuing. Everything else comes second.

And finally, to my Lord and Savior Jesus Christ. You are the love of my life! Without you, I can do nothing. All glory, honor, and praise belong to You.

Introduction

Welcome! Over the course of this book, I hope to present you with some things that a good portion of the general population probably has no idea about. Among them are some things beyond imagination and others beyond even explanation. They are, however, things that are relevant to our walk with the Lord, things you may have questioned within yourself but never pursued.

That's where I come in. When I come up with questions, I feel the need to learn the answers! This book was born inside me long before the thought of writing a book even occurred to me.

Many years ago, I began to pray for wisdom and the Lord has been faithful in answering that prayer. I tend to ask the questions that make you want to stop and think about the answer, answers that often require a great deal of study and research to reach conclusions on. I don't just take what is offered up and swallow it. I want to conduct my own research to verify it.

To be honest, I'm not exactly sure anymore what the question was that initially sparked the idea for this book. The manuscript has evolved. It has blossomed into something much greater than I could ever have imagined.

I started out reading a book about Albert Einstein, which led to more books about Einstein, which led to a lot of other interesting subjects. I suppose, like the majority of the population, I had never stopped to ponder the things that make the world what it is today. I mean, we all have an occasional thought about how something happens or works, but rarely do we pursue it any farther than that.

In my first book, *Entering Into the Hall of Faith,* I challenged readers to walk closer with the Lord. In this book, I look to strengthen your faith by providing scientific evidence coupled with Scripture. This book is no way, shape, or form meant to subvert or replace God's Word – it is simply intended to come along side and gird up with natural and scientific knowledge the things that we see around us.

If you are ready to begin, just sit back and you'll hear a tale. A tale of the bizarre and intriguing world as you have never heard it before, a look into Einstein's famous equation, and a foray into the confusing and exciting world of quantum physics!

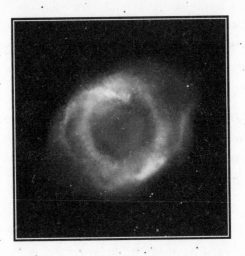

The Eternal Now

Intriguing thought isn't it, the Eternal Now? For those of you who have read my first book, you should have an idea of what that means. Others of you might have no idea what I am talking about. Some of you feel like the circumstances you are currently going through seem to be eternal. Some of you are just curious enough to pick this book up to see what it is all about. Either way, read on.

If I may, let me set the stage for you. This book will attempt to tie Einstein's most famous equation, $E=MC^2$, along with some other scientific theories, together with some spiritual insight from the bible.

The Eternal Now is only one of three sides that we will look at pertaining to Einstein's equation. It also happens to be this book's original title while I was first working on it. The Eternal Now is one of the first things God showed me in relation to science.

The Eternal Now is an intriguing concept based on the speed of light and accounts for more than a third of this book in some shape, form, or fashion, scattered and intricately weaved throughout. As such, it gets special mention at the beginning. As always my heart's prayer for your journey through this book is found in Ephesians 1:17-18:

That the God of our Lord Jesus Christ, the Father of glory, may give unto you the spirit of wisdom and revelation in the knowledge of him: The eyes of your understanding being enlightened; that ye may know what is the hope of his calling, and what the riches of the glory of his inheritance in the saints (Ephesians 1:17-18).

This may seem like a strange question, but have you ever felt like you were living in a snow globe? Maybe not specifically a snow globe, but you felt like you could only go so far before you ran into an invisible wall that held you prisoner. Invisible boundaries that seem to be impenetrable. No matter what you have tried, you just could not seem to get beyond those limits.

Then, without any warning, someone comes along and shakes your world violently. But when all the swirling water and falling snow subsides, you find that you are still bound by the same seemingly impenetrable walls. Well, this time you get a warning. I am about to shake your snow globe with some thought-provoking ideas.

The most historical and scientifically accurate book that has ever been written is the bible.

The possible implications that these insights may have on your life are exciting, to say the least, and potentially explosive enough to shatter the glass wall encasement built around you by traditional education. I hope to change your thought patterns and provoke some insight into the greatest Scientist that ever was, still is, and is to come: our God, Yahweh!

There is a revival taking place in the intellectual community that will have eternal ramifications on the world as we know it. The most historical and scientifically accurate book that has ever been written is the bible, and it's being proven over and over by some of today's greatest minds.

If you can believe my next statement, the rest will be child's play: *In the beginning, God created the heavens and the earth.* If you can believe that one statement, the rest of the bible will be easy enough to believe. Our bible was God-inspired down to the last letter. God's Word is inerrant, infallible, and inexhaustible. Nothing happens by chance when God is involved. He didn't just fling the universe into existence and see what came of it. God didn't roll a set of cosmic dice and end up with you and I. No, everything that **is** was created by Him and for Him for a specific purpose.

That includes you. Do you know what your purpose is? Just like our fingerprints or our DNA, your purpose will be unique to you and no one else can fulfill it.

I want you to read the next sentence and then stop and think about it for a moment before going on. *No one can worship Him like you do.* Now seriously, stop and think about that. You are the only one that can worship God like you do. In fact, there are scientific studies that suggest that the very DNA that makes you up and is unique to you is a song. They have decoded DNA and been able to translate it as music! That means you have a unique song on the inside of you that only you can sing.

I really meant what I said earlier, that you are the only one who can worship God like you can. Your worship is unique, and if you don't worship, then God is missing a piece of worship. Compare it to a symphony with God as the conductor. If you aren't worshipping, there is a empty space in the music. The Conductor may be the only one who notices, but He notices. Your purpose in the Kingdom is just as unique as your worship. Everything in God's creation has a plan, a purpose and a destiny.

I've always been a bit on the curious side. If something puzzled me, I would take it apart and see how it worked, much to the dismay of others at times. If something was broken, I would try to fix it, whether I had any idea what I was doing or not. The complexity of some things amaze me while the sheer simplicity of other things are just as astounding.

> Everything in God's creation has a plan, a purpose and a destiny.

I have a very analytical mind and for years that held me back from understanding God and the things that occurred in the bible. I need for things to make some sense to me. That all changed one day when I heard someone say that God set all the laws of the universe into existence and was bound by them just as we are. He has to work inside the laws that govern our world and dimensions just like we do. Now, while that may be counterintuitive to some of you, that really caught my attention.

Then something was said that really peaked my interest and set me free. Simply put, God is the greatest Scientist that has ever lived. He knows how to supersede the laws that hold in us check. Now that made a lot of sense to me. Suddenly, all the lights came on! I could finally see what I had been missing. This may seem pretty simplistic, but I had never thought of it in quite that way before. God made all the laws and is held accountable to them just as you and me, except that He knows how to work around them.

I'm sure some of you balk at the idea that God is subject to the laws that govern our world, but let me give you an example. We know that God made the earth and everything in it. We know that God made Adam and gave dominion over the earth and everything in it to Adam. We also know that Adam gave up his authority to Satan in the Garden of Eden. If God wasn't bound by the laws of this world, He would not have had to send His Son Jesus into the world as a human to live a sinless life yet die as the lowest of sinners. If God wasn't bound by His own actions, He could have just smacked Satan upside the head and taken dominion of this world away from Him.

He had to do things in such a way that He did not violate His own Word and laws. God began to speak immediately of redemption while Adam and Eve were still in the Garden confessing their sin to Him. He prophesied of Jesus in Genesis, Exodus, Leviticus, Numbers, Deuteronomy, and so forth. The entire Old Testament was written to prophesy Jesus into being. The Old Testament is Jesus concealed while the New Testament is Jesus revealed. The bible is not the history of man, it is the story of redemption of mankind.

It took God four thousand years to get the conditions He needed to send Jesus into the world to take back authority without violating the laws that He set in motion in the beginning. The deeper you delve into studying the bible, the more you realize that God is not only the greatest Scientist but also the greatest mathematician. From equidistance letter sequences to the DNA and the lineage of Jesus, not one word or letter in the bible is without design.

We will talk more about the different technologies mentioned throughout the bible later on. But for now, let's get back to our topic.

Many consider Einstein to be the greatest scientific mind that ever lived, but Einstein only discovered what God had already set in motion. Just as with the airplane, once mankind figured out lift and thrust, we could supersede gravity. After my epiphany that God was, simply put, the greatest Scientist that will ever be, stories from the bible began to run through my mind: Philip being translated from one place to another, Jesus becoming invisible and walking right through the crowd of people who wanted to throw him off the cliff, Elijah calling fire down from heaven, Moses parting the Red Sea, Joshua destroying the walls of Jericho with a shout, Jesus walking on the water … the stories are endless.

Jesus didn't break the law of gravity when He walked on the water. He superseded it somehow that could be explained scientifically, if only we knew what God does. Maybe He changed the atomic lattice of the cells of His body to be the opposite pole of the earth's magnetic field and created an electromagnetic field to repulse gravity so that gravity didn't affect Him. Maybe He changed the composition of the water to hold Him up. Both theories are no more than wild speculation, but with the correct knowledge they could be used to explain how Jesus walked on the water.

God used men and women of the bible to bend or supersede the laws that He had set in motion because He knew exactly what was needed in each situation. That is one of the reasons that obedience is so important. Things may not make sense to us in the moment, but they do to God because He sees things from a different perspective. Not only a different perspective, but a different dimension.

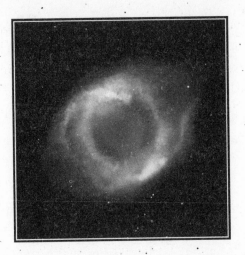

Pause and Perspective

Imagine with me, if you will, a football game. From our first perspective, you are watching it on TV. You have no control over what you see; the view is dictated by the director. He can zoom out the camera so you get a broader sense of the field, or he can zoom in so you focus on one particular player. He can show you forward and backward, sideline to sideline, but he controls all that you see.

This comparison is much like God in our lives. He zooms out sometimes and shows us a broader view of the picture from where we can see more generally what is transpiring on the spiritual battlefield. Alternatively, He could zoom in on the main focus, whoever has the ball at the moment, so to speak. He might show us the wide receiver down field for us to throw the ball to. It's not

It's not about us, it's about being part of a team, or a single Body in Christ.

about us, it's about being part of a team, or a single Body in Christ, and carrying out the plays that the coach calls. In this game, however, there are no audibles! He makes the right call every time! No matter what we think, it is the right call for that play.

Now imagine that our football game is really a three-dimensional holographic image … except we're not aware that it's an image; as far as we are concerned, we are in the holograph playing the game. Sure feels real, right?

Let's say you are the quarterback. You are behind the line and looking for someone to throw the ball to. You are having to look over your offensive line and the defensive line that is trying to crush you. You are in the heat of the battle, making split-second, game-altering decisions. Do you throw the ball or do you run it yourself? You don't see anyone open, so you decide to run the ball yourself to keep from losing ground. You pick up a couple of yards, but when you get back in the huddle, one of your receivers says he was wide open and could have scored.

From your perspective, you couldn't see anyone open, but from his perspective he was wide open. The perspective is different for every player on the field. Every fan in the stands has a slightly different perspective than the person sitting beside them. The coach up in the skybox can see the entire field from his point of view.

Now imagine that the coach is God and He exists outside the game altogether. Since this is a three-dimensional projection, He can pause the game and turn the field in any direction He wants to get a better view of any player. He can see how the play is developing and knows where the players will be in the following seconds. He whispers to our quarterback to throw the ball to the left sideline at the thirty yard marker and restarts the game. Our quarterback still can't see anyone, so does he follow his instinctive inner voice or does he try to run the ball himself?

He throws the ball and out of nowhere comes his receiver, who catches the ball and runs in for the touchdown. We are very much in a holographic situation like the one I have just described. We will talk a little more about this later on.

God hath chosen the foolish things of the world to confound the wise (1 Corinthians 1:27)

It probably didn't make much sense to the people of Israel when Joshua told them to march around the walls of Jericho silently for seven days, and then on the last day to march another seven times and give a blast of the trumpets with a shout of victory. It may not have made sense, but it worked, didn't it? I believe it was a combination of the vibration and frequency made by the marching and the shout that canceled the frequency of the stone and mortar that held the wall together. Can you imagine the vibration caused by that many people marching and shouting to God in triumph?

Satan shares his power with those immature and weak enough to be under the illusion that they are in control. God shares His power with those mature enough to realize that He is in control and He has total reign of their life because they have submitted themselves to His purpose and will. When God has the reins of our lives and can guide us with the slightest pull of the halter, He can trust us with His power.

> God shares His power with those mature enough to realize that He is in control

Jesus had the Spirit without measure because he humbled himself and was obedient, even unto death (Philippians 2:8). When we become obedient to Galatians 2:20 and are crucified with Christ and allow Him to live through us, we will see miraculous things begin to take place as well.

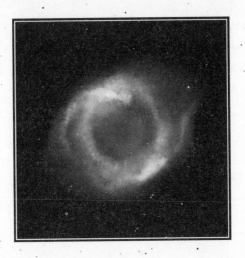

Control Freak

Let's talk for just a moment about the most famous and recognizable math equation in the history of mankind, Einstein's $E=MC^2$. I imagine all of us know what this means, but just for good humor let's assume that no one does and break it down.

If we wrote a sentence problem out of it, it would read like this: The amount of energy in an object is equal to the mass of the object multiplied by the speed of light squared (multiplied by itself), which is equal to thirty four billion five hundred ninety six million. Einstein's theory was that anything that had a mass also had energy.

People that are not as familiar with Einstein as I am may not know that $E=MC^2$ wasn't the original equation that Einstein came up with. The original equation was $M=E/C^2$, which in itself was quite a large step forward for the scientific world, but was nothing compared to the conceptual $E=MC^2$ giant leap that propelled us into the atomic age of science.

To say that this was a revolutionary idea is like saying the ocean is full of water, or the sky is full of stars. In reality, Einstein's equation, the water in the ocean and the number of stars in the sky are all unfathomable!

Einstein's initial formula, published in his 1905 special theory of relativity, was that if you added energy to a mass, the mass would increase by the amount of energy added to it, divided by the speed of light squared. Then he did something simple, something wonderfully, marvelously simple, and rewrote the formula in its familiar form of $E=MC^2$.

The biggest idea in Einstein's equation was that all mass has energy.

The idea came to him that if energy has mass, then mass should also have energy. So the biggest idea in Einstein's equation was that all mass has energy, or that mass and energy could even be considered to be the same thing! The problem with most energy, however, is converting the property of the mass into energy.

For example, the gasoline in your car is a mass that, when converted into energy, powers your car. It is converted into energy by the motor at a rate equal to the demand the gas pedal places on the motor. If a lighted match, which has its own energy, were dropped into a gallon of gasoline, it would also convert that same mass into energy. But it would be a sudden release of uncontrolled energy.

Converting the mass into energy isn't the only problem. Controlling the conversion can be a troublesome prospect. The atomic bombs used to end World War II was the mass of a small amount of uranium (less than one ounce) converted into kinetic energy that was uncontrolled. We all know how destructive that was. (For those who have any knowledge of these events, you may feel I am in error about the amount of uranium used. However, most physicists agree that the bombs used to end World War II used less than 1% of their potential energy. Thus, less than one ounce was actually converted into energy. We will look at this in more depth later on.)

That same amount of uranium can be converted in a nuclear power plant under controlled conditions and provide power for thousands of homes across the country. The difference is the control of the release of energy.

So, the first real relevance that I want you to understand here is that all mass has energy. The second is that to make that relevant, we must find out how to release the energy in the mass or how to convert it into energy. And finally, once we have understanding on how to convert the mass into energy, we must then know how to control the energy that has been converted. Otherwise catastrophes occur and people get hurt. With that in mind, let's take a deeper look at Einstein's equation.

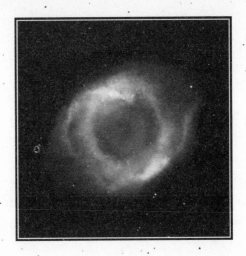

E=MC²

So what does this equation mean exactly? What qualifies as mass? What is the speed of light? What is energy? Let's see if we can answer each of these questions in a simple way.

Mass is anything that can be measured, all the way down to an atom. Even smaller than that is the particles that make up an atom, right down to the electrons and photons. We're talking really small, tiny particles that are billions of times smaller than the period at the end of this sentence.

A photon has zero rest mass because it is always in motion. Since it is always in motion, it obviously has energy ... and therefore has mass, because if all mass has energy, then all energy has mass. The mass of a photon is a relativistic mass, or a mass in motion. So that is a very basic overview of mass.

Now, our next question was: What is the speed of light? The speed of light is considered by most to be a constant 186,000 miles per second. That figure has been rounded off. I believe the exact number is 186,232 miles per second. That's what I call PDQ, or pretty darn quick.

For a very long time, the speed of light was considered to be instantaneous. It moves so quickly that it is very difficult to measure. Imagine that the moon was a very large mirror and that you had a flashlight powerful enough to shine to the moon. The average distance to the moon is 238,856 miles. That means that when you turned on your flashlight, it would take the light from that flashlight one and a quarter second to bounce off the moon mirror and return to earth. That's PDQ!

Of course, our mind really can't even comprehend that distance or speed. In more relative terms, in one second light could travel around the earth at the equator seven and a half times, or across the continental United States sixty-two thousand times! I imagine you can understand now why light was considered to be instantaneous until the last few centuries.

The last part of the equation is energy. Energy is the ability to perform a specified function, or it can simply be defined as a force. I will only mention this in passing here, as we will deal more in depth later, but energy can neither be created nor destroyed. Since the beginning, all energy has existed in one form or another.

Moving on, there are many types of energy that we are all familiar with. The electricity in your house is electrical energy, the gas in your car is chemical energy. I live near a nuclear facility. That is nuclear energy that is transferred into electrical energy that is then sent to my house and becomes light or radiant energy. It also becomes heat or thermal energy through the process of the heat pump by means of mechanical and chemical energy.

This is an example of the energy in our lives everyday. Energy is all around us. The fat cells in your body is energy from the food you ate too much of and became stored and is now potential energy. When we move, it is because of the energy in the food we ate being converted into kinetic energy. I could continue rambling about energy, but I suppose you already grasp the basic concept.

The real implication of the equation is that all matter has an enormous amount of energy bundled up inside of it. The underlying question is, do we really understand the dramatic consequences that this equation has on our ordinary, mundane, seven-days-a-week, twenty-four-hour-a-day lives?

The most common misconception is that Einstein's equation is useful only as a nuclear threat or in a nuclear reactor that creates electricity. No one thinks about how it applies to normal activities. Not a day goes by that this little equation isn't at work in even the smallest things we do. If the equation itself had a mass, it would have to be a relativistic mass because the equation is always at work. It is never at rest.

Even the very thought pattern required for reading this book is a result of the equation. Every breath you take, and every move you make, $E=MC^2$ is watching you. The very framework of this world's existence is a direct result of Einstein's equation. Not that the world we live in is a result of the equation, but that the equation is the result of the intelligent design of the universe.

It is a very simplistic, basic understanding of how everything works. When we learn to apply this natural understanding, combined

> The very framework of this world's existence is a direct result of Einstein's equation.

with spiritual knowledge and revelation, we will be able to see that they are one and the same. The only difference is that they are in different realms. It is God at work in everything at all times. It is His faith-filled words that is the energy in all mass.

Has anyone ever heard of zero point energy? Zero point energy is when you take a cubic centimeter of empty space (that's roughly the size of a sugar cube), pull a vacuum on it (so that it's completely devoid of any matter), and drop the temperature to absolute zero (or 274 degrees below the freezing point of water). In that cubic centimeter of completely empty, very cold space, there is energy just churning away! Exactly how much energy? Well, that's still being debated. Some say there is very little energy, while I heard one say that there is the energy of a hundred million of our suns in there. At any rate, everyone agrees that there is energy at work in the midst of nothing. Does that seem odd to you? I believe it is this energy that holds together the very atomic structure of atoms. I believe it is this energy that even allows the universe to exist!

*Through faith we understand that the worlds were framed **by the word of God,** so that **things which are seen were not made of things which do appear*** (Hebrews 11:3).

God's Words are the very fabric of the universe! Everything that is seen and unseen was framed by the Word of God. Scientists have spent billions of dollars to discover what a $10 bible could have told them. Recent studies have "established beyond any doubt that a fraction of a second after creation, the universe was filled with tremendous energy in the form of wildly moving exotic particles and radiation. Within a few minutes, this energy employed E=MC^2 to transform itself into more familiar matter – the simplest atoms …"[1] Do you realize

God's Words are the very fabric of the universe!

what those scientists have discovered? The first Words recorded from God.

And God said, Let there be light (Genesis 1:3).

When God said, "Let there be light!", what He set in motion was not the sun. We know that light in the context we are talking about existed before the separation of light and darkness because He didn't set the bodies to rule over the day and the night until verses 15-18. What He spoke into existence in the midst of the darkness was, "Let there be the Knowledge of God!"

The entrance of thy words giveth light*; it giveth understanding unto the simple* (Psalm 119:130).

When God spoke into a dark, void, and formless world, the entrance of His words was light. That light was filled with the faith of God that was, is, and will forever be the energy that scientists have recently discovered existed a fraction of a second after creation. It actually existed before creation as well, but they haven't figured that much out yet.

God's word says several times in the New Testament that His words will never pass away! Now here's a bit of a brain teaser for you: What day during creation did God create the plant life? I already told you this one, but what day did God separate the light from the darkness and create the sun and moon? The answers are that He created plant life on the third day and the natural light on the fourth.

Does anyone find that a bit out of order? What do plants need to live? Light and water. So obviously the plants got what they needed from the first "light" that God spoke into existence, not from the sun. Well, I hope you're sitting down while you read this, because I can tell you that it will be so again. In Revelation 21 and 22, we discover that there will be no need of the sun because Jesus, the Lamb of God, will be the light. Now that's the kind of Son burn I want! I want to be a reflection of His light for others to see.

We were talking earlier about the fact that all energy has mass. With that thought, think with me for a moment. Sound is a form of energy, correct? We've all heard of sound waves. Sound waves are a form of energy. Have you ever heard someone say that someone's word carried a lot of weight? I've got news for you, then. So does yours! Your words have a mass and a frequency. If you speak God's Word full of His faith using the same frequency He spoke, they carry as much weight as they did when God spoke them.

The opposite is also true. If you don't speak God's Word over the same situation, but instead speak your own ideas and negative, fearful thoughts, you speak death and destruction with a frequency that cancels out faith. No matter how many people pray for you, if you are speaking fear and doubt, you are speaking a frequency that is canceling out faith. James said our tongue is like the rudder on a great ship. Such a small member guides the entire vessel! We must get hold of this one thing, that life and death are in the power of the tongue (Proverbs 18:21).

This, of course, sets the stage for our next topic.

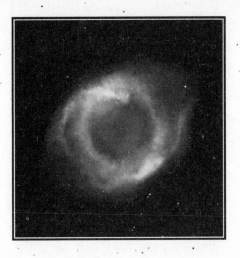

Constants

Several scriptures tell us that God's Word will never pass away. That's a long time! Of course, it's really not a long **time** at all, but we'll discuss that further a little later on. For now, let's say that it is an indefinite expanse outside of time altogether. Jesus even tells us that not one jot or tittle will pass away (Matthew 5:18). A jot and tittle is the equivalent in our language of dotting our i's and crossing our t's. There is an old rabbinic saying that when Yeshua comes, He will not only open the meaning of Scripture to us but He will also interpret the letters, punctuation, and even spaces between the words. And yes, I believe the Word is literally that layered and precise.

So what exactly classifies as a constant? The dictionary says that a constant is "something always present or available, occurring or made again and again, remaining the same, or faithful." In mathematics, it represents a fixed value.

We know that Jesus is the Word of God and Jesus said, *I will never leave thee nor forsake thee* (Hebrews 13:5). Jesus is always present and available. God's Word is a constant! He is omnipresent. *For as in Adam all die, even so in Christ shall all be made alive* (1 Corinthians 15:22). And we know that it is *in Him [that] we live, and move, and have our being* (Acts 17:28).

It is because He is alive that we even exist. His Words are still occurring and causing us to be, this very nanosecond, or we wouldn't exist. The frequency of His voice is creating us again and again, faster than the blink of an eye. It is His *immutability* (Hebrews 6:17) that allows us the freedom to know that He isn't going to change the rules midstream. We don't serve a schizophrenic God. His very name is *Faithful and True* (Revelation 19:11). And we know that we are not our own for we have been bought with a price (1 Corinthians 6:20). That price was the priceless Son of God, who lived a sinless life in love and fulfilled all the law and the prophets (Matthew 5:17). God and His Word are constant.

> We don't serve a schizophrenic God. His very name is *Faithful and True.*

There are many things that are considered to be constant in this world. Most people would consider time to be constant, but we will see shortly that Einstein disproved that with his theory of relativity. Most scientists believe that the speed of light is constant. Einstein himself believed this, but it has been shown of late that the speed of light is slowing down. This is known as the variable speed of light, or VSL theory for short. There was an article in Scientific American in its June 2005 issue that stated that, if the speed of light is slowing down, our entire three-dimensional world is only a "shadow of a larger reality."

Wow! Even the scientists are starting to catch on. This world is definitely only a shadow of a much larger reality. They have no concept of just how profound their statement was. The blockbuster movie *The Matrix* may be closer than any of us are willing to admit!

Everything in our world is made up of atoms, which are a digital simulation of the things they make up. They are nothing more than a binary code blinking yes or no, on or off. The entire universe is nothing but a shadow of a much, much larger reality. The physical realm is not real! It is temporal and will pass away.

The spirit realm is the real world that will always be! The physical realm is comparable to the matrix in the movie. It is only once you have been awakened to the real world that you can see it for what it is. I only wish it were as simple to download information into us as it was in the movie, although I have heard stories of missionaries being called by God to specific nations and instantly knowing their language!

For those of you who haven't seen the movie, I do recommend you take a look at it through these parallels. I love the line where Morpheus is teaching Neo how to operate in the matrix and Neo says, "Are you telling me I can dodge bullets?" Morpheus replies, "No, I'm telling you when you know who you are, you won't have to!" When we come to the realization of who we are in and through Christ, the devil will not be on the offensive anymore; he will be on the defensive.

We have often heard the scripture telling us that the gates of hell will not prevail against you (Matthew 16:18). Since this is Jesus speaking, I am going to take Him at His Word. Gates are a defensive weapon, right? You've never seen a gate attack anyone, have you? No, they are meant to keep things in or out. Upon the revelation that Jesus is the Christ, the Son of the living God, the gates of hell will not prevail. Whether we are attacking them from inside to escape spiritual Egypt or we are on the outside going in to help those that have been held in bondage, the gates of hell will not prevail.

Okay, enough movie analogy. Let's get on with our constants.

There are many other things that are considered to be constant. For example, each element in the periodic table has a constant atomic frequency. But I submit to you that there is only one constant in the universe: the Word of God! Written and spoken, the eternal, always present and available, occurring right now, never changing, faithful, priceless, constant Word of God! How can I say that? Because I happen to believe His Word.

Surely everyone knows the first scripture from Genesis. *In the beginning God created the heaven and the earth* (Genesis 1:1). If you can't believe the first verse in the bible, you won't be able to believe any of it. If you can't take by faith the premise that God created the universe, then you can forget understanding the rest of the bible. Because it is *through faith we understand that the worlds were framed by the word of God, so that things which are seen were not made of things which do appear* (Hebrews 11:3).

It is through faith that we can even understand the bible's very first verse. Everything that we can see was not made of things which are apparent, but was formed and fashioned by the very Words that flowed from God's mouth. *All things were made by him; and without him was not any thing made that was made* (John 1:3). That verse is my stance that God's Word is the only constant in the universe. All things, seen and unseen, macroscopic and microscopic, were made by Him.

The table of elements has an atomic frequency that sings the glory of God because He spoke the table of elements into being! I met a man, Mr. David Van Koevering, who was instrumental (pardon the pun) in building a piano-type instrument called the RoyEl. Named after the man who conceived this device, Roy Wooten, the RoyEl is an instrument that plays the frequencies of the periodic table of elements.

Roy Wooten of Bela Fleck and the Flecktones, also known by the name Futureman, claims to have seen this device before he had it built. David Van Koevering and Bob Moog have changed the musical world with the instruments they have created. David was having heart trouble and physically died twelve different times before his heart was repaired. It was during one of these times when he says he was "falling into light" that he could hear sounds he had never heard before. Not long after that, he was to speak at the intermission where this instrument that plays the table of elements was being debuted. To a group of his peers, he wept as he explained that he had heard those same frequencies as he was passing from this realm into the spirit realm. He heard the same sounds coming from that invention as he had when he lay dead and crossing over. That's because the RoyEl is playing audibly the voice of God speaking the elements into existence. As David was between the two realms, he also heard God's voice speaking the physical realm into existence.

Remember earlier when we talked about Joshua canceling the frequency of the walls of Jericho with a shout? Everything in creation has a frequency and is resonating with the voice of God that spoke it into existence. That is how we can move mountains. By changing the frequency of an object, you alter it. Let me give you an example of this. Gold has a frequency. If you apply the frequency of a hot enough flame, it will alter the frequency of the gold, which then becomes a molten liquid with a different frequency. However, as the gold cools off, the frequency changes again as it returns to solid form.

God's Word has a Master frequency, so to speak, that when it is spoken with the authority and faith of God, changes the frequency of what is being spoken to. I bet you could even make a piece of iron swim if you wanted to. What's that? That's ridiculous you say? Iron can't swim! Preposterous! Really? You might want to check out the story of Elisha and the floating axe head in 2 Kings 6 before you laugh too hard.

When we speak the Word of God with the authority and faith of God, creation recognizes Whose words are being spoken and obeys.

> When we speak the Word of God... creation recognizes Whose words are being spoken and obeys.

Joshua stopped the sun because he spoke with the authority and faith of God. Jesus calmed the storm by speaking peace into it with authority and faith, not just because He was the Son of God.

When the church gets out of the identity crisis it's been walking in and sees itself as it really is, the Body of Christ, we will speak and the elements will have to obey God's voice spoken through us! God's Word is the only thing in the universe that is constant. While other things in this world are considered to be constant, it is my belief that they are only constant because God's Word is still resonating through them and causing them to be.

Personally, I believe that's why there isn't a logical explanation for the double slit experiment that was first performed by Thomas Young. This experiment creates quite a paradox for us. It tells us that light is both a wave and a particle. How can it be two different things at the same time? Is it a wave or is it a particle? The answer is, yes, it is. If you've never heard of this paradox, you might think I'm quite delusional. But I assure you that many others have tested this and come up with the same results.

In 1906, J.J. Thomson won the Nobel prize for proving that electrons were particles. But in 1937, his son was awarded the Nobel prize for proving that electrons were waves! There is a great deal of research now that gives compelling evidence that electrons only manifest as particles when we are looking at them! If that doesn't upset you, you weren't listening to what you just read!

Let me see if I can explain the double slit experiment. I encourage you to look up this information on the internet, because a picture of this really is worth a thousand words. If a single photon of light is expelled, then it shows as a particle, but when it combines with other photons, it shows as a wave, or photons bumping into each other and acting randomly. Well, that is actually simple enough to understand and seems to be a logical explanation.

What about the fact that if you shoot individual particles at a single slit on a screen, they all act as particles and form a line on the second screen behind the first screen? But if you open two slits and fire individual particles, they act as waves. Now there's nothing for them to "bump into" and cause the randomness of a wave, and yet they do. Somewhere between where the particle is fired and the first screen, our particle observes whether there are one or two slits and determines how it wants to act.

Now, you have to look at that as rather odd. You might not even believe what I'm telling you. It's nature's magic! If you really want to get weird, picture this. If we conduct the exact same experiment, but this time we set up a camera that is capable of capturing which slit our particle comes through, we will be able to observe its behavior. This experiment has actually been done, by the way. Now we fire our individual particles at the first screen with only one slit open. As expected the particles act as particles. Now we open our second slit and fire our individual particles again. Finally, we can understand how they act as waves, right? Nope. With our camera observing the experiment, behind the first screen but in front of the second screen, the particles all act like particles! They know we are watching them!

Let me give you one more little surprise. You think the camera has somehow interfered with the experiment, so let's leave the camera in place but turn it off. The camera is still there but it is turned off. Again we fire at will the individual particles with both slits open, and this time they act like a wave! They know the camera has been switched off! It's as though they enjoy tormenting us by keeping their little secret. The only thing that has changed here is the observation. I guess our particles had the feeling someone was watching them. Maybe they are camera shy. Or maybe you just have to take some things by faith.

Quantum mechanics has been proven over and over, but no one really understands the why's of it. Richard Feynman's most famous quote about quantum mechanics is, "I think it is safe to say that no one understands quantum mechanics… in fact, it is often stated of all the theories proposed in this century, the silliest is quantum theory. Some say that the only thing that quantum theory has going for it, in fact, is that it is unquestionably correct." Well, that should clear things up for you.

Four years before Einstein's death in 1951, he wrote a letter to Michele Besso, a dear friend, and said, "No one really knows what light is! All we know is that it can be both a particle and wave. And that's the paradox. How many things do you know of that can be two different things at exactly the same time?"

I believe that light is equivalent to the Body of Christ. As an individual we are pinpoint particles and when we walk in unity we create a wave. Our destination and actions should be at His sole discretion, and should be carried out without being observed by others. Whether we are a pinpoint particle or a part of the wave is up to Him. In fact, I propose that we can be both. We can be a part of the wave and still be a pinpoint particle in someone's life without observation, even our own observation. We thought we were just surfing the wave of the Holy Spirit, but someone on shore may be watching without you even knowing to see if you wipe out or ride the wave. **Be** a witness for Christ at all times. Only when necessary or led by the Holy Spirit should you use words.

The question used to haunt me that we are here, yet we are seated together in heavenly places in Christ. How is that possible? You can't be in two places at the same time! Or can you? Time is the factor that does not allow it. Imagine, if you will, that time only exists in one of those places. That puts a whole new spin on it, doesn't it? You can be here at a set time and be in another dimension where there is no time simultaneously!

Enter the Eternal Now. We live so three-dimensionally conscious that we rarely acknowledge time as the fourth dimension anyway. Then this concept shouldn't be that hard for us to grasp.

Let me see if I can explain this concept a little deeper. The three dimensions that we recognize easily are length, height, and width. In other words, the normal 3-D world we live in. The desk my laptop is sitting on is five feet wide by thirty two inches tall by thirty-six inches deep. These are all relative terms we are used to dealing with.

Now, let's say I set my computer here for a twenty-four hour period. I come back tomorrow and move my computer upstairs to the coffee table. The three dimensional space that my computer was taking up is now unoccupied, because it was only there for twenty-four hours. Time is our fourth dimension and a physical property. The space that was previously my computer could now be a glass of water and a stapler. The space is the same, but the time is different. Time is the only thing that prevents A) my computer being on my desk and on the coffee table at the same time, and B) my computer, glass of water and stapler all occupying the same space at the same time.

From this simple example, we see that time is the only relevant factor. I hope that gives us a rather simple grasp of the time and space correlation. Now imagine the exact same space, but without time. My desk is just sitting there in a fifth dimension where time hasn't stopped, it simply doesn't exist! Now my office is really in five dimensions at the same time! Three that create the space, one that dictates time, and another where time doesn't exist. Now my computer can sit on my desk in the fourth dimension of time and my glass of water and stapler can exist in the same space simultaneously in the fifth dimension where time doesn't exist. The space that was previously my computer could now be a glass of water and a stapler.

Jesus said the kingdom of God is at hand. It's not off in outer space somewhere, it's right here, **in another dimension**. I met a man in Coeur d'Alene, Idaho who is a quantum physicists and fellow brother in Christ. David Van Koevering teaches on what he has come to call "Elsewhen". It's not in another place; it's in another time. Actually, I believe it is outside of time altogether. We keep waiting for Jesus to come rescue us from this miserable place and take us away. Truth be told, we aren't going very far. We're just going to another timeless dimension that is parallel to the world we live in.

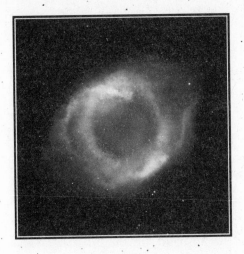

Time Keeps on Slipping...

I suppose with all this talk of time vs. timelessness we should go ahead and start looking at the ramifications of Einstein's equation, along with his previous and subsequent theories. According to Einstein, time stops at the speed of light.

First, let's talk about time a bit. For the most part, time rules us. We have schedules that tell us when to be where and at what time. We have calendars, date books, palm pilots, PDAs, blackberries, watches, and any number of other devices that serve to remind us to do things on time. Someone asks us to grab lunch with them, and we say, "No, I don't have time today." We get busy and look around at the clock, "Where did the time go?" We have a lot of sayings regarding time:

According to to Einstein, time stops at the speed of light.

Have you got a second? Time flies! Will this day ever end? Do you have the time?

But there are two kinds of time. There is subjective time, the way we perceive it internally, and there is objective time, the way the clock ticks. Subjective time is the way that we view how time passes. Imagine a husband and wife going out to see a movie. Not just any movie, a chick flick of all things! In the theater, the wife gets all wrapped up in the plot and gets emotionally touched by it. She is so involved in the movie that nothing else matters. No outside thoughts are bombarding her. She is completely invested in the characters and their outcome. The husband, on the other hand, just can't seem to pay attention. He couldn't care less about the movie. He's just there to pacify her. He's really not following the story at all. He's thinking about what he could have been doing instead. When that wears old, he gets sleepy and nods off a couple of times only to jerk back awake.

After the movie, they go out to eat with another married couple. The wives excuse themselves to the ladies room. One of the greatest mysteries in the universe is put into motion at this point. Why do women go to the ladies room in pairs? Is it left over instinct from Noah's ark? Safety in numbers? The world may never know. Regardless of why, the ladies are in the restroom powdering their noses when one says to the other, "You have got to go see that new movie! It was wonderful. I just couldn't believe how it ended." The other wife asks, "I'm not sure Bill would sit through it. How long was it?" The first woman thinks for a moment, then says, "Oh, it wasn't long at all. Probably just over an hour. It was over before I knew it."

At the same time, back out at our restaurant table, Bill and Fred are discussing the same topic. Fred tells Bill, "Do *not* go see that stupid movie! It was so boring, the biggest possible waste of my time.

I didn't think it would ever end. That was one of longest movies I think I've ever seen. It must have been three hours."

Here's a good example that most people can identify with. To her, it seemed to be just over an hour, while to him it seemed like an eternity. Truth be told, the movie was exactly two hours long. In subjective time, to her it flew by and to him it was a long, steady torture that dragged on and on.

Subjective time is relative to the observer only. It is how we *feel* time passes in our own mind. Objective time is how everyone views time. It is the clock on the wall, ticking by ever so steadily. Seven days a week, twenty-four hours a day, thirty-one million five hundred and thirty-six thousand seconds a year. Objective time is how we measure our subjective time. It is the yard stick, so to speak, that determines a unit of time. A second, a minute, an hour, a day, a month, a year, a decade, a century – all are increments of objective time. Objective time told us the movie was exactly two hours long.

Objective time never changes, right? Time is constant. Well, our brilliant mind Einstein would disagree. He believed that time is relative to the observer and to motion. Hence, he didn't believe in space and time separately anymore, but rather space-time. If only all those scientists would study the bible, they would have had revelations like these hundreds of years ago.

One of the problems is that our English language isn't always as descriptive as it should be. The Hebrew and Greek are much more expressive and precise. For example, if you look at time in your

> If only all those scientists would study the bible, they would have had revelations like these hundreds of years ago.

concordance, there are nineteen different Hebrew words used in the Old Testament that are translated as *time* in English. Each of those nineteen words has a different meaning, but in English it just means *time*. That is why we have to carefully discern every word written, rightly dividing the Word of God.

Let's look at an example of that.

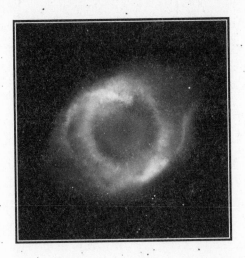

Deep Thoughts

*But thou, O Lord, shalt endure for ever; and thy remembrance unto all generations. Thou shalt arise, and have mercy upon Zion: for the **time** to favour her, yea, the set **time**, is come* (Psalm 102:12-13).

If we look carefully at these two verses, we see that there are actually five references to some kind of time there. We have the phrase that says the Lord will "endure for ever." That one is easy enough, since we know that God will be around for ever. The actual Hebrew word there means eternity.

Remembrance is our second time reference. Remembrance is a covenant word. Any time you see remembrance concerning the Lord, stop and remind yourself that He is talking about the covenant between God and man. Consider the Lord's Supper in this frame of reference. *This do in remembrance of Me* (1 Corinthians 11). Remembrance refers to an event that has occurred at a specific point in the history of mankind. Although it refers to a past event of man, with God it is as though the covenant is being made at that moment.

A good example of this occurs in Deuteronomy. *But thou shalt remember the Lord thy God: for it is he that giveth thee power to get wealth, that he may establish his covenant which he sware unto thy fathers, as it is this day* (Deuteronomy 8:18). Approximately seven hundred and twenty-five years had passed from the time God swore this to Abram in Genesis 15 until this point where God is reminding them to remember Him and His covenant with them. Seven hundred and twenty five years is a long time! But if you noticed the last part of that verse, in God's eyes it is **as it is this day!** It is still the Eternal Now with God! His covenant with Abraham is as fresh on His mind now as it was the day He swore it.

If you understand this fact and know the benefits of this covenant, it should excite you because we are the heirs of that covenant through Christ! His covenants are always on the forefront of His mind. It is us that has to "remember" Him. The covenant in Genesis 15 is also an unconditional covenant. If you are not familiar with this passage, I encourage you to study it out. In a normal covenant ceremony in that day, they committed the sacrifice and laid out the animals just like Abram did back in Genesis. The two parties would then walk back and forth through the blood in a figure eight, symbolizing infinity, and state the terms of the covenant. In this instance, however, God causes a deep sleep to fall on Abram and God alone walks through the blood and declares the terms of the covenant. That makes this a one-sided declaration. The only condition necessary to be a beneficiary of this covenant is to be a seed of Abraham! This gives us an idea of remembrance in our Psalm 102 verse.

The reference in Psalm 102 to generations is unique because it refers to all generations. Normally, a generation is considered to be forty years, a specific generation. In this instance, it refers to past, present, and future generations, or an age of generations. That's three references relating to time so far.

Then, if you read carefully, we have two actual mentions of time. *Thou shalt arise, and have mercy upon Zion: for the time to favour her, yea, the set time is come.* Let's look at the first time mentioned here. In the original Hebrew, the word used here is "eth", which means **time conceived as an opportunity.** I love this definition! This is the way we should perceive our day every morning when we wake up. Our entire life is time conceived as an opportunity, an opportunity to live for God and to worship the King of kings and the Lord of lords! He loves the fact that we are so loyal to His doctrines, but He prefers to have our devotion. In other words, God likes all the things we do for Him, but we can get so busy doing things **for** Him that we never spend any time **with** Him.

> God likes all the things we do for Him, but we can get so busy doing things **for** Him that we never spend any time **with** Him.

The second time mentioned here is "moed", which means an appointed place of meeting, or a particular time and place. That has a surprising correlation between space and time, doesn't it? That sounds a lot like space-time to me. Time and place in the same context. We've often heard of being in the right place at the right time. Well, here it is. So that puts a new spin on things. We also know that when we see Zion mentioned, it represents the church.

So with all our new found knowledge, let's look at that verse translated a little closer to the original meaning. *But You, O Lord, will endure for eternity! And Your covenant will stand till the end of this age. You will arise and have compassion on Your Church, for there is an opportunity to favor her, for the appointed space-time is come.*

This melds well with the space-time theory, doesn't it? The idea of a particular place at a specific time. As we see, though, that specific time can be a period of thousands of years with God. It can also be a set time of much smaller proportions. In Genesis, when God is talking with Abraham about the birth of his son Isaac, God uses this translation three different times, in Genesis 17:21, 18:14, and 21:2. Go ahead and look at those individually. Each one is speaking of Isaac being born at a specific space-time.

In the New Testament, the equivalent would be a "kairos" moment, a specific space-time in God's calendar of events. This is also a reference to our fourth dimension. Paul even prayed for us to be able to comprehend other dimensions in Ephesians.

*Ephesians 3:14-18 For this cause I bow my knees unto the Father of our Lord Jesus Christ, of whom the whole family in heaven and earth is named, that he would grant you, according to the riches of his glory, to be strengthened with might by his Spirit in the **inner man; that Christ may dwell in your hearts** by faith; that ye, being rooted and grounded in love, may be able to comprehend with all saints what is the **breadth, and length, and depth, and height** (Ephesians 3:14-18).*

Our inner man and Christ dwelling in our hearts is an allusion to another dimension of our eternal spirits. A fourth dimension is actually listed in verse 18. There is breadth, length, height, and **depth**. God alluded to this in the Old Testament when He said that His ways are higher than our ways – not just because we don't understand His ways, but that His ways have more than three dimensions. Several more.

Beloved, now are we the sons of God, and it doth not yet appear what we shall be: but we know that, when he shall appear, we shall be like him; for we shall see him as he is (1 John 3:2). We could paraphrase that to say that we do not yet know what we will be like, because we do not understand the dimensions that He exists in. But when He appears, we will be like Him and we will see Him and understand all the dimensions.

It is now believed by particle physicists that as many as ten dimensions exist, but that only four are measurable. Nachmonides, in his *Commentary on Genesis*, published in 1263, determined from his extensive study of the creation account that there were ten dimensions, but that only four were knowable.[9] Imagine that. Again we see that what took scientists until recently to discover, after spending billions of dollars on particle accelerators, had already been written about hundreds of years ago through a careful study of the bible.

After His death, burial, and resurrection, Jesus could enter and exit a room without passing through any of the six planes that created it. He didn't pass through the four walls, floor, or ceiling. He passed through a different dimension. Now, here in Ephesians, we actually see a fourth dimension mentioned. In the Greek, depth is "bathos", which means profundity and mystery. The immeasurable depths of God's wisdom and knowledge, a place where hidden wisdom and mysteries dwell, is a dimension all its own.

> The immeasurable depths of God's wisdom and knowledge... is a dimension all its own.

We know all things are hidden in Jesus, *in whom are hid all the treasures of wisdom and knowledge* (Colossians 2:3). The Father has to reveal things at specific space-times to Jesus as well. Ludicrous, you say! To confirm this, let's look to Revelation 1:1.

The Revelation of Jesus Christ, which God gave unto him, to shew unto his servants things which must shortly come to pass; and he sent and signified it by his angel unto his servant John (Revelation 1:1).

It doesn't get much clearer than that. God revealed unto Jesus the revelation that He is. Another scripture that mentions the dimension of depth is found in Romans. *O the* **depth** *of the riches both of the wisdom and knowledge of God! how unsearchable are his judgments, and his ways past finding out!* (Romans 11:33). It's the same depth mentioned in Ephesians.

Some things science may never figure out in this age. Some things are beyond our finding out. Some things you have to take by faith in order to explain certain other things. If we could explain everything, it wouldn't take any faith, now would it? But everything that is can be explained scientifically by the One who created it, if He so desires.

The same word used as depth in these two scriptures is also used to describe the depth of the soil in the parable of the sower. I could go into a long spill here, but to keep from straying too far off course I'll paraphrase the parable. I encourage you to read this account in the Gospel of Mark, verses one through 20, and study it in depth, because Jesus says if we don't understand this parable, we won't be able to understand any of them.

The seed in the parable is the Word of God. The sower goes out and sows seed. Some falls on the wayside and the fowls of the air devour it. This represents the Word of God sown in those who haven't received Jesus. Before it can have a chance to germinate, demonic forces come to stop it. These seed are sown in everyday encounters with people we meet and speak into their lives, knowingly or unknowingly.

The next group we see represents the point I'm talking about. The sower sows some seed on stony ground, or hard hearts. These people know Jesus as savior, but that's about it. They haven't worked at knowing

God. Maybe someone presented the Gospel of Jesus to them and got them saved but didn't go on to tell them more. Jesus says that because they have no **depth of roots**, the seed is scorched and withers away. They have no knowledge or wisdom in the things of God. They haven't discovered that next dimension of God's word. It is line upon line and precept upon precept, so layered that we could never understand it all with human reasoning.

His Word is inexhaustible! The depths of God are what we draw out of when the heat is applied by the enemy. Hosea 4 tells us that God's people are destroyed by a lack of knowledge. That is essentially the same thing that Jesus says here in Mark. Because they lack root depth, or knowledge, they are destroyed.

The rest of the parable is that the sower threw some seed among thorns and it was choked out by them. This crowd is the worldly in the church. They have more world in them than God. They apparently have at least some depth, or they would have been classified and lumped in with the previous group that had no depth of root. It is my speculation that these were at one time on fire for God and digging into His word. Unfortunately, what they have heard taught from the pulpit and decided to try hasn't worked in their lives. The true Christian lifestyle is not a trial and error scenario that evolves and gets better and more sophisticated over time. It has to be a life-altering, unchangeable decision that, if it is in God's Word and can be corroborated by other scripture, it is Truth that must be followed. The seed that fell on this ground had some depth, but I believe they lacked patience ... therefore lost their promise. They know too much to go back strictly into the world system, and so they straddle the fence. Hence, the weeds and thorns choke out God's Word.

The last group is the seed sown on good ground. Those who are not straddling the fence, those that run off the demonic, those that have depth in their hearts. They produce fruit with patience.

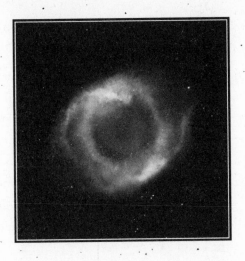

It's About Time!

Let's get back to the issue of time. Einstein showed that light was relative to motion in the special theory of relativity, that no matter how fast the observer was traveling, the speed of light was always the same. That doesn't compute with our normal logic. Normally, if Sally is driving in her car at 60 mph and Susie is driving in the same direction in her car at 40 mph, then Suzie would see Sally pulling ahead of her at a rate of 20 mph. But that isn't the case when we deal with light.

Of course, we aren't dealing with normal speeds, so we'll have to go outside the box here to even imagine this. If Sally were in her rocket car speeding along at 93,000 miles per second, half the speed of light, and a beam of light shot by her at the normal 186,000 miles per second, then it should appear to her as traveling 93,000 miles per second faster than her. But that isn't the case. To you and I standing by motionless, it would appear that way – but not to Sally. To Sally, the beam of light would still be traveling 186,000 miles per second faster than her. How can that be?

Well, if the speed of light is constant in the equation relative to both Sally, who is traveling half the speed of light at 93,000 miles per second, and myself standing idly by, the only other thing relative would be time inside Sally's rocket. This was counterintuitive in Einstein's day and not very well received. He should have received the Nobel prize for his work on the special theory of relativity, but it was a little too "out there" for most people. How could time not be constant? This led Einstein to believe that if you could travel at the speed of light, time would stop. We know from the Word that God is light. Here are a few examples of that.

The Lord is my light and my salvation (Psalm 27:1).

Who coverest thyself with light as with a garment (Psalm 104:2) Note the mention of light as a garment in the next verse as well.

And was transfigured before them: and his face did shine as the sun, and his raiment was white as the light (Matthew 17:2). Again, what follows is the mention of light and His garment.

In him was life; and the life was the light of men (John 1:4).

*This then is the message which we have heard of him, and declare unto you, that **God Is Light**, and in him is no darkness at all* (1 John 1:5).

So if God is light, then He must travel at a speed equal to or greater than the speed of light that we know. Most likely at a speed much greater than our known speed of light. The fact that God travels at a speed greater than the speed of light would also explain why He is omnipresent, or everywhere at the same time.

Now hang with me for just a minute and let's see if I can explain what I am feeling. God already exists outside of time. We have established that much. We know that God is omnipresent, but that isn't simply because He exists outside of time, because the rest of the Spirit realm is outside of time also and yet we know from scripture that the angels and demons and Satan can only be in one place at a time. They have a locality, so to speak. Therefore, simply being outside of time doesn't get us to being omnipresent. There has to be another factor involved.

At the speed of light, time simply stops. But if God travels faster than our speed of light, and He wanted to go from here to South Africa, He would arrive there before He left here. Much like the elusive tachyon, our computers can't find it, because if we run a test looking for a tachyon traveling faster than the speed of light, the result of our test shows up before the test began. Wow! God is the only being that can travel above the speed of light. The angels and demons can only be in one place at one time and would therefore travel at or below the speed of light.

Again we can say that God exists outside of time. And if God exists outside of time, there is no past or future. There is only the Eternal Now. And if there is only the Eternal Now with God, and He arrives in South Africa before He left, then He could be back and somewhere else and would never have left the Eternal Now! He could be everywhere at once and never have actually left. Selah! Think on it.

God is the only being that can travel above the speed of light.

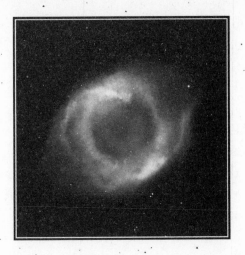

Are You Washed in the Blood?

Since there is no past or future in God, we begin to understand why certain scriptures can be true.

*There is therefore **now** no condemnation to them which are in Christ Jesus, who walk not after the flesh, but after the Spirit* (Romans 8:1).

If there is only **now** in Christ Jesus, then that is why there is no condemnation for us here and **now.** We could just as easily say that there has never been, there is not **now,** nor will there ever be any condemnation in Christ Jesus. If Jesus didn't exist outside of time, then we would still be in condemnation. When He died and rose again in another dimension, outside of time, He took a quantum leap. David Van Koevering would say He popped a quiff. That is why He can wipe our sins away like they never happened. He just steps back to the point in our time when we accepted Him and the Blood washes our sins away.

This has to drive Satan absolutely bonkers. He works so hard to get people deeper and deeper into sin. To quote C.S. Lewis from "The Screwtape Letters", he knows that the "safest road to hell is a gradual one." He doesn't expect you to go to hell in a hand basket overnight. He plants seeds of lust or thoughts of perversion and then waters them with more thoughts, dragging you deeper into the thought of it each time. Eventually, you've thought on it so long that you take a small step. Maybe you look up a softcore website or buy a Playboy magazine. Then, before long, that doesn't do it for you anymore so you find a hardcore website or a XXX magazine. You develop a fetish of some kind and eventually end up having an affair, raping an innocent person, or even becoming a child molester. He would love nothing more than to get you to harm a child, because that is another life that he can then prey on.

Truth be told, he has quite a diabolical plan laid out to keep you moving deeper and deeper into sin. Still, he doesn't have to push people very hard. Our flesh enjoys such things and wants to do them. Once he has his hooks in you, he can lead you like a fish with just a slight tug on the pole, all the while reeling you in. No one starts out in life to become a child molester or a rapist. It happens slowly without their even noticing how far they have fallen.

> All it takes to be set free is for you to come to call out for Jesus. That has to infuriate Satan.

But there is good news. The deeper you get and the farther you fall, the more you realize you need Jesus. All it takes to be set free is for you to come to call out for Jesus. When you do that, with one drop of Jesus' blood, it is all erased! That has to infuriate Satan. It would be like building a magnificent sand castle and then having the tide come in and wash it away, removing any trace of it ever having existed. Isn't God awesome?

I still remember the only open vision I have ever had in my life so far. I was only nine years old at the time. It was a cool, brisk morning and I was watching for the school bus. Our house faced south and the school bus arrived from the east. I was leaning up against the wall, looking out the window, as I saw the clouds begin to stir, sort of rolling and billowing. It was like nothing I had ever seen clouds do naturally.

And then Jesus stepped through the clouds and stretched out His arms. Not necessarily toward me, but toward the world. Behind Him three crosses appeared on a hill, and from the hill flowed a river of His Blood. The river flowed toward me until it ran off a cloud embankment and created a waterfall. I could see people in the river of blood being washed over the waterfall. They were all laughing and enjoying the experience. Then, just as quickly as it had all appeared, it was gone.

I'm not talking about seeing something vague or indistinct. I'm talking about watching the biggest plasma screen you could imagine! The colors were vibrant and everything was crystal clear. I thought the rapture had taken place and I missed it. I wasn't afraid when I saw it; it was afterward that a reverential fear of God came on me. I forgot all about the bus after that. I immediately went to find my sister to make sure I wasn't alone. I didn't quite grasp the rapture completely at that age.

I can tell you that to this day, that morning is still very real to me. I get goose bumps sitting here recounting it for you. A true encounter with God will leave a marker on you that you can recall anytime without hesitation.

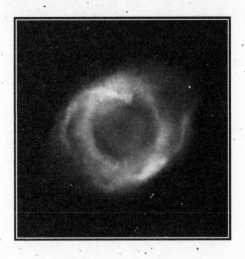

Back in Time

Once again, back to our subject of time. By the way, just that small phrase, "subject of time," is interesting. Most of us are subject to time, but time is subject to God. Joshua made time his subject once when he caused the sun to stand still. You can read that story in Joshua 10. The bible says there has never been a day before or since like that one. It was basically one day that was 48 hours long. Several different cultures have tales of this encounter, too, so the bible isn't the only source to corroborate the story. For example, there is a tale in the Far East called The Long Night of China. I had never really thought about the effects this event would have had on the other side of the world until I heard of China's

Now that we know God exists outside of time, we can see why He is the same yesterday, today, and forever.

long night. Historically, the two events even occurred around the same time.

Now that we know God exists outside of time, we can see why He is the same yesterday, today, and forever. We can also begin to glimpse the idea that He is the beginning and the end, but at the same time (forgive the figure of speech) has no beginning or end. That is still an odd idea, I know, but things are seldom what they seem when you first observe them. We can get a glimpse of why He never changes but is always changing in our perception of Him. We can also glimpse why He said in Hebrews that *now faith is the substance of things hoped for, the evidence of things not seen* (Hebrews 11:1).

With **now** faith outside of time, we can step back into the spirit realm and the Eternal Now and create whatever it is we need with our **now** faith. It took thousands of years before Einstein had the revelation that energy and matter are one and the same. "It may take a few more years before we prove that wisdom and knowledge are the basis of, and can actually create, energy which in turn creates matter."[2]

Your **now** faith is the raw material that can create the energy which is also the matter you need. John 1 gives us a good overview of Genesis and the creation account. *In the beginning was the Word, and the Word was with God, and the Word was God. The same was in the beginning with God. All things were made by him; and without him was not any thing made that was made* (John 1-3). God created everything we see and don't see with His **now** faith. When we realize that we are seated together in heavenly places in Christ Jesus, we too can create with our **now** faith.

I mentioned earlier that there are several different Hebrew words that were translated as time in our English bible. By far the most common of those in the Old Testament is one that I mentioned earlier. Namely, "Eth", which means time conceived as an opportunity. Our time here on earth is nothing more than an opportunity to love Him and to worship Him by choice, to see His Kingdom come and His will be done, on earth as it is in heaven.

We know from the Word that the angels have the ability to make choices. This is evidenced by the fall of one third of the angels. While they may certainly have the ability to make choices and decisions of who they are going to worship, they do not have the right to make those decisions. They were created by Him for Him. They don't have the freedom of free will like you and I do. Of course, they are also in His manifest presence. How hard is it to worship God when you are in His manifest glory?

You and I have a time here on earth that is our conceived opportunity to worship Him by our free choice. You wouldn't want your kids being nice and loving on you just because they had to or wanted something. No, you want them to spend time with you because they love you. The same is true in a marriage. You don't spend time with your mate because you have to, you spend time with them because you want to. Or at least I do.

> Our time here on earth is nothing more than an opportunity to love Him and to worship Him by choice.

Once we cross over to that dimension, it won't be very hard to worship Him. It means so much more when we are still on this side, walking through the fire, unable to see Him in all His splendor, walking by faith with the praises of God on our lips all the while. Worship in the wilderness is a sacrifice and sweet savor to God.

We all go through wilderness experiences. My nephew works for me in my construction business. Whenever I have a difficult or dirty task, I tell him he gets to build some character. The tough times are the character building times. Take for example an antique fighting sword. The steel was heated to the point where it was pliable and then pounded into shape. It was then heated again and again, each time folding and compressing the blade materials together and beating any air bubbles or impurities out of it. I have heard that some swords had as many as a hundred folds! But without this process, the sword would be useless because it would not be hardened enough to withstand the battle.

We, too, must be willing to go through the heat and pounding process in order to be able to fight in the good fight of faith and not be broken and destroyed. **Now is our opportunity**, our opportunity to be fashioned into His image and likeness.

In Luke 4, the recollection of Jesus' temptation in the wilderness, our priorities are set in order for us. Let's look at verse 6-8. *And the devil said unto him, All this power will I give thee, and the glory of them: for that is delivered unto me; and to whomsoever I will I give it. If thou therefore wilt worship me, all shall be thine. And Jesus answered and said unto him, Get thee behind me Satan: for it is written,* ***Thou shalt worship the Lord thy God, and him only shalt thou serve*** (Luke 4:6-8).

These are our priorities! Worship first and service second. Your devotion to the King can keep you so busy that you forget to spend time with the King. We can become so involved with ministry that we forget to sit and spend time with the One we are ministering for. Our first call is to minister to Him through our worship. God wants our devotion, but He wants our worship and adoration and undivided attention above all else.

A good example of this is the account of Mary and Martha. *Now it came to pass, as they went, that he entered into a certain village: and a certain woman named Martha received him into her house. And she had a sister called Mary, which also sat at Jesus' feet, and heard his word. But Martha was cumbered about much serving, and came to him, and said, Lord, dost thou not care that my sister hath left me to serve alone? bid her therefore that she help me. And Jesus answered and said unto her, Martha, Martha, thou art careful and troubled about many things: But one thing is needful: and Mary hath chosen that good part, which shall not be taken away from her* (Luke 10:38-42).

We see here that while Martha was busy playing hostess and serving everyone's needs, Mary chose instead to sit at Jesus' feet and hear His words. Jesus said that Mary chose the good part and it would not be taken away from her. Martha was so busy ministering that she neglected Jesus in the way that He really enjoyed the most, simply sitting before Him and enjoying His presence. It is in these times that we will receive our instruction and guidance for the ministry He has for us.

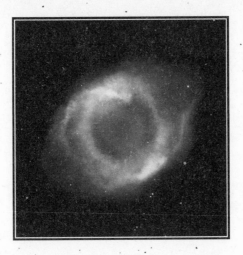

Eternal Now Covenant

And I will establish my covenant between me and thee and thy seed after thee in their generations for an everlasting covenant, to be a God unto thee, and to thy seed after thee (Genesis 17:7).

I am going to have to assume that you know about the covenant to at least some degree, or that you will study about it in Genesis 12-22. I can only go into so much detail here without writing a whole book on the subject. We see here in Genesis 17 that God makes a covenant with Abram that is not just for him, but for his seed after him and their generations. This is the same generations that we saw earlier in Psalm 102:12 – not to a particular forty-year generation, but to all generations that are of Abraham's lineage. The point we see here is that Gods tells us that this is an everlasting covenant to all of Abraham's seed. All of the generations that come out of Abraham were included in this covenant.

Now to Abraham and his seed were the promises made. He saith not, And to seeds, as of many; but as of one, And to thy seed, which is Christ (Galatians 3:16).

This makes it sound like all of the promises stopped with Jesus. But that isn't the case! If we look back just a couple of verses, we see otherwise.

That the blessing of Abraham might come on the Gentiles through Jesus Christ; that we might receive the promise of the Spirit through faith (Galatians 3:14).

That sounds better, but it still makes you think that we may have just inherited the Spiritual promises through Jesus and not the actual covenant that God swore to Abraham. To clarify the point, let's look at one more verse.

And if ye be Christ's, then are ye Abraham's seed, and heirs according to the promise (Galatians 3:29).

That's pretty straightforward. No room for argument there. If you have accepted Jesus, then you are considered Abraham's seed through Christ. Let me encourage you to study out the covenant of Abraham on your own. You should understand that if you are Abraham's seed and heirs of the promises that God made to him, then you have to know what those promises are in order to take full advantage of them. It would be like knowing you inherited a bank account with a million dollars in it but never bothered to find out the account number. Without the proper knowledge, either is useless. There is a lot of information in the bible about the covenant, easily enough to write a book about it. Alas, not at this space-time.

Let's look at a couple more scriptures before moving on. We referenced this scripture earlier, but it bears repeating.

Deuteronomy 8:18 *But thou shalt remember the Lord thy God: for it is he that giveth thee power to get wealth, that he may establish his covenant which he sware unto thy fathers, as it is this day* (Deuteronomy 8:18).

This is God's perspective on our covenant with Him through Jesus Christ. If you notice again the end of this verse, it says *as it is this day.* In other words, with God being in the Eternal Now, it is as though He is back in Genesis 15 swearing the covenant with Abraham at any and every moment. Next, I want you to see how seriously God takes His promises. He doesn't make flippant promises like humans do.

For when God made promise to Abraham, because he could swear by no greater, he sware by Himself, saying, Surely blessing I will bless thee, and multiplying I will multiply thee. And so, after he had patiently endured, he obtained the promise ... Wherein God, willing more abundantly to shew unto the heirs of promise the immutability of his counsel, confirmed it by an oath: that by two immutable things, in which it was impossible for God to lie, we might have a strong consolation, who have fled for refuge to lay hold upon the hope set before us (Hebrews 6:13-15,17-18).

God doesn't break His promises! Not ever! But He went a step above that in this covenant to Abraham, and you and I. God made a promise to Abraham and then, on top of that, He swore an oath on His own name, because there was nothing greater to swear by. If this covenant ever fails, then God will have to step off His throne and cease being God! He swore on His reputation as Creator of the universe.

God doesn't break His promises!

Now, you might be thinking, "Then why aren't those promises working in my life?" If you look back, you will notice that Abraham had to patiently endure until they came to pass. Abraham was seventy-five years old when God first promised him a seed. He was one hundred when Isaac was born. Could it have been hurried along? I don't think so. God mentioned three different places in Genesis that Isaac would be born at a specific space-time. It's not a what we want, when we want it kind of thing, which sets the stage perfectly for our next topic.

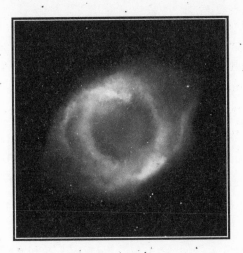

Wanted: Dead and Alive

We were talking earlier about being in two places at the same time. Is it also possible to be in two states at the same time? I'm not talking about being in Alabama and Texas in the same instant; I'm talking about a state of being. For example, can you be hungry and full all at once? Can you be pregnant and not pregnant? Can you be in faith and in fear at the same time? The answer to any of these is obviously no.

Now, my question is this: can you be dead and alive at the same time? Surprisingly enough, yes, you can. The term for this in quantum mechanics is **superposition,** in which a particle is in two possible states at the same time. For an extreme example, imagine that a particle was a snow skier. It could take the lift to

> Can you be dead and alive at the same time? Surprisingly enough, yes.

the top of the mountain and then take two different slopes down at the same time, yet end up back at the lodge as a single particle. Our particle skier could tell us what both slopes look like, even though it only traveled down the mountain once!

When dealing with something that is in superposition, it is not a here or there condition. **It is a here and there situation.** Jesus gave us the command to be in a state of superposition. He told us that we were to be in the world, but not of the world. His prayer to the Father in John 17 says that we are in the world (in verse 11) but that we are not of the world (in verse 14).

Now if we be dead with Christ, we believe that we shall also live with him: knowing that Christ being raised from the dead dieth no more; death hath no more dominion over him: For in that he died, he died unto sin once: but in that he liveth, he liveth unto God. Likewise reckon ye also yourselves to be dead indeed unto sin, but alive unto God through Jesus Christ our Lord (Romans 6:8-11).

Don't forget the theme we are talking about here. If we keep it in context, we see that we can be alive in this dimension and be dead in the Eternal Now. Or would that really be the other way around? We would be dead to this world and be alive in the Eternal Now in Christ Jesus. In actuality, I suppose we would be in superposition twice, once in each realm. We are called to be dead to this world, but to allow Jesus to live through us for all to see. In the Eternal Now, we are called to be crucified with Christ, yet in Him we live and move and have our being. We find another good scripture for this in Galatians.

*I am crucified with Christ: nevertheless I live; yet not I, but Christ liveth in me: and the life which I **now** live in the flesh I live by the faith of the Son of God, who loved me, and gave himself for me* (Galatians 2:20).

When we accepted Jesus as our Lord and Savior, we stepped back in time, nailing our sins to the cross with Christ and popped the quiff of sin in our life.

And now, back to our particle that was in two states at once. We know that it is in superposition and in two states at once, **however**, once we try to observe it, it becomes a localized particle and only in one place. Until it is observed, it is in a state of non-locality. Just like the two slit experiment we discussed earlier, observation changes everything.

In Matthew 5:28 Jesus tells us, *That whosoever looketh on a woman to lust after her hath committed adultery with her already in his heart.* Even Jesus taught quantum physics. He just told us here that it is the observation that is a sin, not just the deed. There is a lot more to that statement that we don't understand yet, but I believe it will be revealed in the appropriate space-time.

But the good news is that when Satan tries to go back and observe our sin and show God what we did wrong, we have a collapse of the wave function. We can't be in sin and in Him at the same time, so we can only be observed as in Him.

If you understood what I just said, that will make you want to jump up and down for joy. We crucified our self with Him the moment we accepted Him in another dimension. But we are still alive in this dimension. We are dead to sin being crucified with Christ, nevertheless alive and living in the flesh. Jesus said in Luke 9 that if we are going to follow Him, we will have to deny ourselves and

> That means every day we have to get up and nail our ambitions, our dreams, and our goals to the cross.

take up our cross daily. That means every day we have to get up and nail our ambitions, our dreams, and our goals to the cross and say, "Not my will, but Your will be done in my life."

What can I do so that Your Kingdom comes to earth as it is in heaven? Me, my, and I have to die. Him, His, and He are to live through us. Not that He doesn't want us to have dreams and achieve things, but we have to submit those things to Him and allow them to happen in His timing. Psalm 37:4 says that if we delight in the Lord, He will give us the desires of our heart. That doesn't necessarily mean that He will give us what we think we want. We might desire a million dollar house. But after we have submitted our desire to Him and follow after Him and not that million dollar house, I can guarantee that your desire will change. He will give you a new desire of your heart.

That is what the scripture really means. He will give you the desires of your heart, and then He will supply them. Instead of a million dollar house in this realm, you would be satisfied with a quarter million dollar house and want to build a children's home in South Africa for children who don't have anything, or a house to keep young girls from being sold into sex trafficking in Moldova where they can learn a trade and learn about Jesus. Those are just a few examples from my own personal desires.

The church here in America has a warped sense of being. Even now as I write this, there are ministries being investigated for misuse of funds, buying things like toilets and tables for tens of thousands of dollars. That will be for God to judge, not me. Christians think God is their piggy bank for me, my, and I. Most Christians can't afford to give into the Kingdom because they are so deep in debt. We need to quit playing the lottery

Christians think God is their piggy bank.

with God by paying our tithes and waiting for our winnings to roll in. When we worship Him and fall in love with Him for who He is, and not for what He can do for us, we will begin to see things happen for us.

God's name isn't Hugh Hefner. Or, to put it another way, just because God has wealth and power and you say you love Him and pretend to be intimate with Him, that doesn't mean you get to live in a big house and drive a nice car. God knows the intentions of the heart, and as long as you are seeking what He can do for you instead of seeking Him, you'll never get it.

The church needs to stop trying to seduce God out of His blessings and teach the world how to follow after His heart and not His wallet. For too long, ministers have sounded like credit card commercials. God doesn't care what's in your wallet, it's your heart He's after! God said to take no thought for tomorrow. He feeds the sparrows, He'll feed you.

Let me climb down off my soap box now. But I can tell you that when you truly seek God's heart, your desires in this world will change. I'll be glad to see the day when I can give 90% of my earnings away and keep only 10% instead of the other way around. We saw earlier in Deuteronomy 8:18 that God gives us the power to get wealth so that He can establish His covenant. That doesn't mean that we live in the biggest houses and drive the nicest cars and everyone sees us and how good God is to us and wants to be a Christian because of our money. Sadly, that teaching is out there.

When we take care of the world like Jesus told us, the world will see the LOVE OF GOD and be drawn. For God so loved

God doesn't care what's in your wallet, it's your heart He's after!

the world that He gave His Only Son Jesus. Money won't fix the problems in the world, but money combined with the Love of God will.

I can just hear the defense in this case. Well, God loves me so much that He wants me to drive a Bentley! Really? He loves you enough to drive a Bentley and doesn't love that child living in the streets of Moldova selling her body to get food? Does he love you more than the orphans in South Africa and India that don't have enough to eat? No doubt God wants us to have nice things, but it sure appears that we want us to have nice things more. Why not buy a $50,000 car instead of a $100,000 car and give the remainder to spread the Love of God?

I know, I said I was getting off my soap box. Does that mean you don't give into the ministries? No, but you give into the ones that are under full disclosure and don't have anything to hide. Make sure you are sowing into good ground. God gives seed to the sower. If you don't plant anything, you aren't going to reap anything.

Enough said, moving right along.

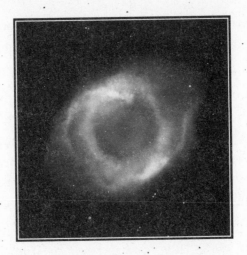

Now That's Massive!

According to Einstein's equation, $E=MC^2$, we see that all mass has energy. Even a small mass has a phenomenal amount of energy trapped inside it. While 52 kg of uranium is required to reach critical mass, physicists estimate that the atomic bombs used on Hiroshima and Nagasaki used about one-tenth of one percent of their explosive capabilities! Less than one ounce of uranium was converted into kinetic energy when the bomb was dropped on Hiroshima and Nagasaki. The blast was caused by a chain reaction of the fission of uranium 235. This is accomplished by shooting a neutron into the atom of uranium 235 and it splits other neutrons off of the original atom into other 235 atoms and repeats the process over and over. Each time an atom splits off,

> Even a small mass has a phenomenal amount of energy trapped inside it.

it generates energy, and when enough have spilt, the bomb is one big ball of energy that is out of control.

All of this typically takes place in a millionth of a second. I don't want to bore you or go too deep into the chemical reaction, but a basic understanding is helpful. The hard part to wrap our heads around is that all mass has that same amount of energy trapped inside it. It is the one ounce mass that produces energy, not only in uranium, but in a golf ball of even in the book you are holding. In anything with one ounce of mass, there is the same potential energy that was unleashed in those atomic blasts.

In May of 1955, Time Magazine ran an article about Albert Einstein called "The Death of a Genius". In that article, the statement is made "that an ounce of matter – sand, oxygen, uranium – holds within itself as much energy as that given off by the explosion of 875,000 tons of TNT." Now, please stop and think about that for a moment. One ounce of matter, 1/16 of a pound, contains the equivalent energy of 875,000 **tons** of TNT. Any one ounce of mass! A regulation golf ball weighs 1.62 ounces. That golf ball would have more than one and a half times that much energy!

To further expand your mind, let's look at TNT a little closer. Trinitrotoluene, for obvious reasons shortened to TNT, is considered a high explosive. There is a common misconception that dynamite and TNT are the same thing, but they are not. One gram of TNT when "triggered" produces one liter of gas. That's a one thousand fold increase in volume. Considering that there are twenty-nine grams in just over an ounce, our golf ball would be equal to just over forty-five grams. Since a golf ball could have the same explosive power as TNT, we can conclude that it would produce forty-five liters of gas, or forty-five thousand grams of gas! That's pretty powerful.

But consider again the statement that an ounce of matter contains as much energy as 875,000 tons of TNT. That's the equivalent of 1.75 **billion** pounds of TNT in just one ounce of matter. There is enough energy in one gram of matter to power a 100 watt light bulb for over twenty-eight thousand five hundred years! That means our golf ball could power forty-five 100-watt light bulbs for over twenty-eight thousand five hundred years.

Earlier, I said that Einstein simply discovered what God had already set in motion. Einstein discovered that all mass has a tremendous amount of energy in it. Where did all of that energy come from? Out of the mouth of God. That tremendous amount of energy that exists inside all mass is the Word of God that spoke it into existence! And all of that energy will respond to the faith of God and be converted into the energy needed to fulfill His Word when spoken by you and I with His faith.

For as the rain cometh down, and the snow from heaven, and returneth not thither, but watereth the earth, and maketh it bring forth and bud, that it may give seed to the sower, and bread to the eater: so shall my Word be that goeth forth out of my mouth: it shall not return unto me void, but it shall accomplish that which I please, and it shall prosper in the thing whereto I sent it (Isaiah 55:10-11).

Einstein simply discovered what God had already set in motion.

This tells us that God's Word will not return to Him void. Our words are carriers of energy, either life or death, blessing or cursing. We should all know that by now. God's Words will not return to Him unless they are full of faith, the energy that He spoke them with when He caused this world to be. God has a no-return policy on His Word unless it is in original condition. When we speak His Word full of faith, it will cause the last half of Isaiah 55:11 to come to pass. It will accomplish that which I please, and it will prosper in the thing that I sent it.

And Jesus said unto them, Because of your unbelief; for verily I say unto you, If ye have faith as a grain of mustard seed, ye shall say unto this mountain, Remove hence to yonder place; and it shall remove; and nothing shall be impossible unto you (Matthew 17:20).

I know that this has been taught over and over, but there is so much that has been left unsaid. Why did Jesus say that if we had faith **as** a grain of mustard seed? Because that mustard seed is a mass, albeit a small one, and Jesus knew that their was enough energy in the mass of that mustard seed that when it is mingled with the faith of God, it would move that mountain from one place to another. Our faith is the trigger.

Remember the atomic bomb we mentioned earlier? Just one neutron started the chain reaction that caused the enormous explosion. When we pull the trigger, our faith rushes into the energy inside the mass that we are speaking to and causes a chain reaction. The faith of God that spoke the matter into existence, which is the energy inside it, becomes excited by the faith that we have released into it and performs the task we have told it to. No wonder Jesus said if we had faith **as** a grain of mustard seed, we could say unto the mountain be removed and it would obey.

Our faith is the catalyst for the equivalent of an atomic blast when we release it with purpose. It is strength with direction, power under control, a burst of energy with focus. David Van Koevering says that faith is not a capacitor that can be charged up by good works and then discharged for your miracle. I happen to agree with him. Faith is seeing the situation the way God sees it and speaking the will of God into it. However, if we never spend time in His Word and find out how He sees things, we will never see things the way He sees them. One of the fruits of the Spirit is faith. The closer we walk with Him, the more we will take on His nature.

Joao Magueijo made what struck me as a profound statement in the book *Faster Than the Speed of Light*. In it, he said, "The tremendous amount of energy harnessed inside one gram of matter passes unnoticed because it is never released into the world; it's just like a huge reservoir of energy sitting inside a body, never making its presence known."

What profound insight. That's the reason I can say that there is nothing that you need that God hasn't already provided for in this world. It is simply a matter (pun intended) of releasing the energy inside the matter of whatever it is that we need to fulfill the need. Instead, we allow all the energy in the universe to sit passively by, unused, untapped, unnoticed.

Tremendous amounts of God's energy are sitting uselessly by, held back by what we think of as the Hoover Dam. In reality, it is held back by the skin of a balloon, waiting for a pinpoint particle of faith to pop it and release the flood of energy inside.

For (even the whole) creation (all nature) waits expectantly and longs earnestly for God's sons to be made known (waits for the revealing, the disclosing of their sonship), for the creation (nature) was subjected to frailty (to futility, condemned to frustration), not because of some intentional fault on its part, but by the will of Him Who so subjected it – (yet) with the hope, that nature (creation) itself will be set free from its bondage to decay and corruption (and gain an entrance) into the glorious freedom of God's children. We know that the whole creation has been moaning together in the pains of labor until now (Romans 8:19-22, AMP).

All of creation is moaning, vibrating, pulsating, waiting for the energy inside it to be...put to use.

All of creation is moaning, vibrating, pulsating, waiting for the energy inside it to be spoken to with God's faith and put to use. Do you have any idea how frustrating that would have to be? To have such greatness locked up inside of you, realizing it's potential, but unable to put it into motion without an outside force opening the door? Creation is waiting for our faith to open the door and take dominion. Releasing it into its full potential, its assignment.

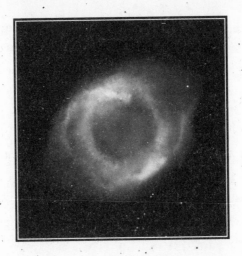

The Cosmic Speed Limit

By now, we've had a pretty good look at the fact that mass has energy. Next, let's look at the idea that mass can never travel at the speed of light, and why that is believed to be true.

According to Einstein's calculations, the more velocity an object has the more mass it has, requiring more energy to propel it. As an object reaches closer and closer to the speed of light, its mass grows larger and larger. According to Einstein, a mass traveling at the speed of light would have an infinite mass. Thus, an object can never travel at the speed of light because an infinite mass would require an infinite amount of energy to propel it. All the energy in the world couldn't propel something as small as a penny to the speed of light, because as it approached what is believed to be the cosmic speed limit, it would achieve an infinite mass.

There are, however, things believed and allowed by physics to travel faster than the speed of light. The tachyon has never been proven to exist, because if it travels faster than the speed of light and if you ran a test to find it at 12:00 pm, the result would show up before the test ever started! A cause without an effect, so to speak. Scientists have a real problem with that. I believe they do exist, but that story will have to wait for another time.

We know from scripture, mentioned beforehand and numerous other places, that God is light. If God is light, then He travels at a speed greater than the speed of light that we currently recognize. Lucifer was the light bearer before the fall. When he fell, the speed of light slowed down and we lost part of our bandwidth. I'll leave this to someone more qualified to explain. David Van Koevering will cover this subject in some detail when he publishes his book, *Elsewhen*. Van Koevering knows a thing or two about light and sound and matter and memory. He truly is an amazing man.

We know that light is slowing down. That much can, and has, been proven. Barry Setterfield and Trevor Norman have performed tests with some amazing results in this field. By measuring the speed of light during eclipses in different years and studying tests performed during previous years, they have been able to determine that the speed of light is slowing down. If it is slowing down now, then we can assume that it used to travel faster than it does now. If you take the measurements and find the rate at which it is slowing per year, and work backward through time applying that same rate of decrease over a period of a few thousand years, you discover that light possibly was many, many times faster than it is today. Some speculation is as much as 10-30% faster during the time of Christ, twice as fast during the reign of Solomon, four times faster when Abraham walked the earth, and as much as 10 million times faster prior to 3000 B.C.

This would be entropy in effect. This could account for the difference in the calculations of creation in the bible versus those of scientists who believe the universe is billions of years old. If light was traveling much faster than it is now and we calculate the distance of a star as being 20 billion light years away based on today's speed of light, your distance is fine, but it is the number of years that you have calculated that is going to way off. Waaaaaay off. I know that sounds like heresy to the scientific community, but one day they may catch up with the bible. Seeing as they're starting with a preconceived notion that is wrong, how could they ever hope to achieve the right results?

J.B.S. Haldane's truest statement may have been, "I have no doubt that in reality the future will be vastly more surprising than anything I can imagine. Now my own suspicion is that the Universe is not only queerer than we suppose, but queerer than we can suppose." That sounds like God to me. Didn't God already tell us that He is *exceeding abundantly above all that we ask or think* (Ephesians 3:20)? John Archibald Wheeler made a similar statement. He said, "We will first understand how simple the universe is when we recognize how strange it is."

> While the world as we know it has become familiar and nonchalant, the quantum world remains a mysterious and wonderful place.

While the world as we know it has become familiar and nonchalant, the quantum world remains a mysterious and wonderful place. I sometimes feel like Neo in *The Matrix* when studying the quantum world. I feel like I took the red pill instead of the blue pill and have fallen down the rabbit hole. As I fall, I wonder just how deep the hole goes. Hey, I think I just saw Alice and the Mad Hatter having tea!

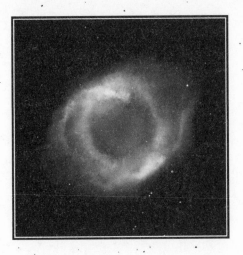

Weight Watchers

If anyone was paying attention, you may have noticed that I have contradicted myself. I said that nothing can travel at or above the speed of light, but I have also said that God travels above the speed of light. Those two ideas oppose each other. Or do they? I also said the reason that nothing could travel at the speed of light was because it would have an infinite mass, requiring an infinite amount of force to propel it. The implication here is that if you could propel an object at the speed of light, it would have an infinite mass and thus an infinite amount of energy.

That's easy enough to fix. We know that God has an infinite amount of force or energy and can therefore travel at or above the speed of light. God =

How much energy does God have? We'll never know because the math doesn't work.

Infinite Energy = Infinite Mass. How much energy does God have? We'll never know because the math doesn't work. If you have an infinite mass or an infinite amount of energy, the rest of the equation is a moot point. God's little finger is traveling at the speed of light and therefore has an infinite mass and an infinite amount of energy. The mass of a body reflects its energy content.

Now that's an interesting statement, considering that we are the Body of Christ. If we are the Body of Christ, then we have the fullness of God, all of His energy at our disposal. Our energy content as His body is the same energy content that spoke the universe into existence and the same power that raised Jesus from the dead!

For it pleased the Father that in him should all fullness dwell (Colossians 1:19).

For in him dwelleth all the fullness of the Godhead bodily. And ye are complete in him, which is the head of all principality and power (Colossians 2:9-10).

Based on the two scriptures above, we can draw the conclusion that in Jesus dwells all the fullness of God. All of the power, all of the wisdom. There is nothing in this world, or out of it, that the secrets of which are not hidden in His Word Jesus. When we are in Him, we are complete. Nothing held back, nothing lacking. All power, all honor, all glory, all praise belong to Him.

In Genesis, we see that on the seventh day, God rested. Do you think God was tired from six days of creating the universe? Do you believe that God had a power drain during those six days and needed to replenish His energy with some Gatorade? I don't think so. I believe what God implemented there was that on the seventh day, creation rested. Under the law, man was supposed to rest on the seventh day. God declared that Israel should farm for six years and allow the land to rest on the seventh year. It had nothing to do with God needing a coffee break. God has an infinite energy supply.

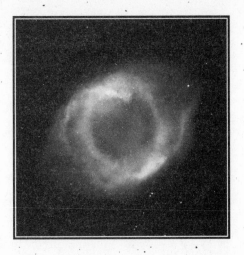

Show Me Your Glory!

If you remember, the idea that mass and energy are one and the same is also known as the Mass to Energy Equivalence. If mass has energy, then energy also has mass. Let's talk about that for a moment. In the book of Exodus, in Chapter 33, Moses beseeches God to show him His glory. The Hebrew word for glory there is "kabowd". It refers to the great physical weight, or quantity of a thing, as well as multitude, wealth, honor, reputation, and splendor.

We hear of people throwing their weight around, or how much weight someone has in a position of authority. That's exactly what Moses wanted to know from God. Show me how weighty you are! Show me how much weight you really carry in this universe! That puts a whole new perspective on the scenario, doesn't it? In essence, Moses said, "I need to make sure you've got my back. If there's ever any trouble, I want to know just how powerful you really are. Show me!"

That's a pretty brazen statement, but it's really not any different than what Abraham said to God in Genesis 15. God said to Abraham, "I am your **shield** and your exceeding great reward." I believe this statement is the first of two mentions of the shield of faith in the bible. The other, of course, is in Ephesians 6. In other words, God told Abraham, "I am going to protect you and make sure you are more than taken care of. You've got nothing to worry about."

That sounds like a good deal to me. That should constitute a feeling of security and peace. But Abraham turns right around and dares to ask for more. He says, "Yeah, what are you going to give me to prove it? I don't even have an heir!" Again, a pretty brazen statement. It's always important to know who's on your team, so when you need to use them for something, you know their limitations of strength and weakness.

The good news is God's on our side and He doesn't have any limitations! Moses and Abraham just wanted to know who God really was. Moses said, "Show me Your glory!" God said, "You can't handle the Truth!" In essence, God was telling Moses that he couldn't handle it all.

> The good news is God's on our side and He doesn't have any limitations!

Remember that mass has energy and energy has mass. That being true, if an infinite mass has infinite energy, then infinite energy would also have an infinite mass. To keep from squishing Moses like a little bug, God restrained from showing him how much weight He really carries. God said, "For there shall no man see me and live." In other words, "You can't see everything about me and survive it. But there is a place by Me, so I'll put you in there and cover you with my hand. As I pass by, I'll remove my hand and you can see my hinder parts." I believe God showed Moses how much weight He had carried from creation up until that point. I believe that is how Moses wrote the Genesis account. Oh, to be Moses and see what he saw there that day.

I believe God has infinite energy. I also believe that's why we cannot stand in His manifest presence. His infinite power has an infinite mass and weighs on us. It is as though we are being crushed under His presence.

I had a dream once that I was in the manifest presence of God. When I woke up, it was as though I was being pressed into the bed. I couldn't move in my dream, His presence was so heavy, but when I woke up, I couldn't move either. It took about fifteen minutes before I could get out of bed. It was like someone was sitting on me. It was quite an experience. I believe it was similar to what Peter, James, and John experienced in Matthew 17 on the mount of transfiguration. Jesus was transfigured before them (and shone like light), and was talking with Moses and Elijah. While this was going on, they were fine but suddenly a bright cloud of God's presence overtook them and spoke. It was at that moment that it says they fell on their face. I don't believe they lay down to worship in reverence, and I don't believe they had a choice in the matter. I believe the manifest presence of God knocked them down.

It is an awesome thing to come into the presence of the living God. Up until Jesus' crucifixion, only the high priest was allowed into the Holy of Holies where God's presence was in the Ark of the Covenant. Anyone else who went in died. The priest was only allowed in once a year to make atonement for everyone's sin. Only purity could stand before God's presence and live, so he had better be clean when he went in or he was dead, too. They would tie a rope around his ankle so that if he messed up and died before the presence of God, they could drag him out. Because no one could go in to get him.

God's presence shouldn't be taken lightly. It is a weighty situation to walk into. God's presence demands a certain reverential fear. At the appointed space-time of Jesus' death, the temple veil that kept man separated from God's presence was torn apart from the top to the bottom, representing that God had torn it and that man could now come before God without the intercession of the priest. Jesus fulfilled all the laws and the prophets. He is now our intercessor. Now all we need to do is accept Jesus as the ultimate and final sacrifice for our sins.

Nothing God does is by chance.

Nothing God does is by chance. When Jesus was born by birth of a virgin, the veil was torn, a shadow of what was to come. There are so many types and shadows throughout the bible that I doubt we will ever recognize them all in this life. How about the fact that the first Adam got his bride out of his wounded side? Jesus was the second Adam, who also had a wounded side and will receive His Bride. It says that Eve was deceived and ate of the fruit of the tree, but it says Adam was not deceived (1 Timothy 2:14). Adam knowingly ate of the fruit and became sin in order to be with Eve. Jesus knowingly was made to be sin for us (2 Corinthians 5:21).

There are so many intricacies interwoven through the scripture that it is like mining for gold. When I'm alone in my study time, I come out feeling like the richest man in the world sometimes. Its treasures are inexhaustible!

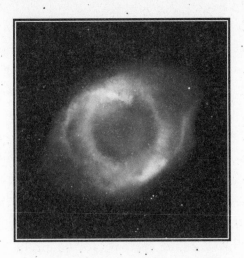

A History Lesson

Einstein was bothered by the idea in quantum mechanics and Werner Heisenberg's uncertainty principle that a system has a definite history. Later, Richard Feynman made an important contribution to physics in his concept of a sum over histories. He suggested an idea that a system didn't just have a single history in space-time, as you would normally assume in a non-quantum theory world. Instead it had every possible history. In other words, you would start at point A, but instead of moving in a straight line to point B, it could take any path.

This is similar to our lives. Everyone asks the question, if God is Omniscient and knows everything, is there really any such thing as free will? Did He know I would be typing this before I did? Did He know whether or not I would accept Jesus as my Lord and Savior? If He did, then wouldn't that be predestination?

We consider that God knows our single history, but what if, like our particle, He simply knows every possible history. In other words, we start our lives at point A, but no other preset course is assumed. There are only options throughout our entire life. From starting point A, we make minor decisions 1, 2, and 3, which leads us to point B. Point B presents us with minor decisions 1, 2, 3, 4, and 5. Each one of those minor decisions leads us to another set of minor decisions a, b, or c … which finally lead us to point C. Every decision leads into subcategories of minor decisions which eventually lead to other major decisions.

It's kind of like deciding to go to a restaurant. In all actuality, the first decision in this process has been made, since you have decided you are hungry and want something to eat. Next, you ask your wife, "What do you want to eat?" I bet most of you guys are psychic and know what the answer to that question is: "I don't care, baby. What do you want?"

Okay, so let's say we have a choice of ten restaurants in the immediate area. First choice, do we eat somewhere close by or do we drive to the other side of town? "I'm tired, let's grab something on this side of town." Now we're getting somewhere. "How about that place next to the house?" I ask. She shakes her head and replies, "No, I had that for lunch." Silly me. I thought she didn't care, right, guys?

Let me see if I can give you an illustration for the typical dinner and the decisions that have to be made for it to occur. This would be a micro example of what the history of a dinner might look like:

Decision #1. I'm hungry! Let's get something to eat.

Decision #2. Do I a) want something in this vicinity, or b) do I mind driving to the other side of town? We choose A.

Decision #3. In this area, we have ten restaurants. Which one do we want to go to? After a lengthy process, we choose a nearby steakhouse. We haven't been to one in a while.

Decision #4. Do we want to eat in or get our food to go? We want to sit down and rest for a while, so we decide to eat in.

Decision #5. We're asked whether we want to sit at a table or a booth. This one's easy. We prefer the privacy afforded by a booth.

Decision #6. Our server comes to take our drink order. Do we want a soft drink? Something from the bar? Ultimately, we keep it simple and decide on waters.

Decision #7. Do we want an appetizer? No.

Decision #8. After looking through the menu, it's time to place our dinner order. There are lots of possibly choices here. Personally, I like the filet.

Decision #9. Since I've ordered a steak, I need to decide how I want the meat cooked. I pick medium.

Decision #10. My meal comes with a side item. After checking out the options, I decide on fries, even though I know the steamed vegetables would be better for me.

Decision #11. What dressing do I want for my salad? So many decisions! I go for Thousand Island.

Decision #12. After waiting awhile, our food arrives. Our server offers us a choice of steak sauces, and I ask for my favorite, A-1.

Decision #13. Now that I've finally got some food in front of me and I've got a mouthful of food, the server checks in on us. "Is everything okay so far?" I nod my head, if for no other reason than my mouth is full.

Decision #14. After dinner, the server suggests some dessert to top it all off. I decline. After all, I couldn't possibly make another decision. Deciding is such hard work!

So, that may have been a bit monotonous, but it should give you a brief idea of the history of a dinner. I bet you didn't realize just how many decisions you make in something as simple as eating out, did you? Imagine now the history of an entire day, a week, or a month! Think of all the decisions, the possible paths that you could take for each choice you make. The list would go on forever!

Does God know every single decision that you will ever make, or does He know every possible choice for every possible decision? The idea is that until it is observed, every possible history would exist at the same time. Only at the time of observation would a definite history become apparent. Could it be that, while God knows all the possible choices that we could make, a definite history doesn't become apparent until we stand before Him to give an account of our lives? That would give opportunity for the Blood of Jesus to step in at any moment and wipe away any history that would be covered by the repentance of sin and the acceptance of Him as Lord and Savior. There would only be two major histories that are pertinent. First, have you accepted Jesus as Lord? And second, did you reject Him? Everything else would fall under one of those two categories.

> **Does God know every single decision that you will ever make, or does He know every possible choice for every possible decision?**

I have come to believe through my studies of quantum mechanics that the emphasis is placed on the observation, not only in quantum physics, but also in the spiritual realm. I believe more revelation will be coming out in relation to the observation of things.

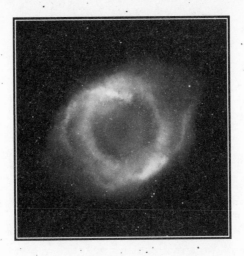

What a Tangled Web We Weave

Entanglement is the single most intriguing aspect of quantum theory in my mind. Erwin Schrodinger named entanglement and defined it as such: "When two systems, of which we know the states by their respective representation, enter into a temporary physical interaction due to known forces between them and when after a time of mutual influence the systems separate again, then they can no longer be described as before."[4]

Here's the simplest definition. When one particle encounters another particle temporarily, they become intertwined. From that point on, whatever happens to one will instantly also happen to the other one, and the distance between them is completely and totally irrelevant! Their fates are, from the moment of entanglement on, dependent on one another. Einstein called this "spooky action at a distance". This idea haunted him and he never really bought into the whole quantum idea. He said, "What nonsense! How obvious it is that quantum theory is inconsistent!"[5] If Einstein had accepted and applied himself to the exploration of quantum theory, I wonder what sort of theories he would have written.

For an example of entanglement, let's use a pair of hypothetical couples. Allow me to introduce you to Will & Suzy and Bill & Lucy. Each couple has been married for about ten years. Will and Suzy live on the east coast in Charlotte, North Carolina, and Bill and Lucy live on the west coast in San Francisco, California.

Suzy has just been promoted at work and has to take a course for her new position at the main corporate office in San Francisco. Suzy was born and raised right there in Charlotte and has never traveled outside of North Carolina. She married her high school sweetheart Bill in their senior year after she found out she was pregnant. She always wondered what life might have been like if she hadn't gotten pregnant, but never talks about it to anyone. She kisses Bill goodbye at the airport and says she'll be home in a couple of weeks. She gets on her first plane, has a drink, and tries to settle in for the long ride. Upon arrival, she takes a cab to the office and reports in for training.

Enter Will into our story. Will is responsible for Suzy's training the next couple of weeks and is enamored with her right away. He and Lucy have been having problems for quite some time now, though are going to marriage counseling. Will calls home and tells Lucy that he is going to have to work late, and invites Suzy to dinner. Rather than eat alone, she takes Will up on his offer. Will and Suzy hit it off and, after a few drinks, Suzy invites Will back to her hotel.

Lucy and Bill, completely oblivious to the goings on, are nonetheless affected by Suzy and Will's actions. Bill and Suzy are one entangled pair while Will and Lucy are another. But we no longer have two distinct pairs, seeing as how Suzy and Will have now become entangled through a temporary physical interaction. Instead, we now have four individuals, or two pairs that are all entangled. Even Lucy and Bill have become entangled through their companions.

Now, if we were dealing with photons instead of people, Bill and Lucy would immediately have known of Will and Suzy's entanglement, along with their own entanglement from across the country, even though Bill and Lucy have never had any type of connection. All four lives have been changed and can never be observed as before Suzy's trip.

The first scripture to prove entanglement is Genesis 2:24: *Therefore shall a man leave his father and his mother, and shall cleave unto his wife: and they shall be one flesh.* Almost everyone has heard that scripture quoted, most often at weddings. But have you ever really stopped to think about it? It wasn't some flippant statement that God made.

Ephesians 5:28-31 tells us, *So ought men to love their wives as their own bodies. He that loveth his wife loveth himself. For no man ever yet hated his own flesh; but nourisheth and cherisheth it, even as the Lord the church: for we are members of his body, of his flesh, and of his bones. For this cause shall a man leave his father and mother, and shall be joined unto his wife, and they two shall be one flesh.*

Not only does this scripture tell us that we are entangled with our spouse, but we are also entangled with Jesus. That's how we can be seated together in heavenly places **in** Christ Jesus.

I am not going to get into a theological debate here, but I want to use another scripture that proves spiritual entanglement. *And I say unto you, Whosoever shall put away his wife, except it be for fornication, and shall marry another, committeth adultery: and whoso marrieth her which is put away doth commit adultery* (Matthew 19:9).

Can you see the tangled web we weave? If you are a virgin when you marry your spouse, and she has been with two guys, who in turn have been with three girls each, who in turn have been with two guys each … I presume you can see where I'm going with this. You carry a lot of people into the marriage with you instead of it just being you and your spouse on your wedding night.

The church often refers to this as "soul ties". It doesn't just apply to the people that you or you spouse have been with. It stretches beyond to the people they have been with and the people those people have been with, and so on and so on. Our government would rather teach safe sex than abstinence. Of course, it isn't the government or the schools' place to teach about either. That responsibility falls to the parents and the church.

Most churches want to talk about homosexuality, but not adultery. That's why our churches are constantly riddled with divorce and scandal. The divorce rate in the church is just as high as it is in the world. Their vow, their covenant, their promises to each other said at an altar, standing before God, a preacher, and witnesses, mean nothing to them. To some brides, it is more about the wedding than being married. And people wonder why the divorce rate is so high!

> **The divorce rate in the church is just as high as it is in the world.**

Thank God for the Blood of Jesus ,because at any time He is standing with outstretched arms, waiting to forgive us of our sins and wipe those entanglements away. It is still a good idea to go through some type of deliverance with someone trained in that area, not only to break off soul ties from previous relationships but any generational curses that may have been passed down from your ancestors.

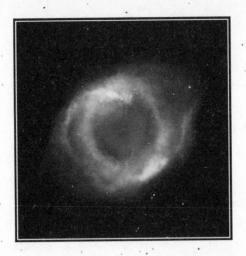

Welcome to the Omni

I would like to take the time now to look at each of the three "omni" characteristics associated with God. I've already mentioned a few of these in previous chapters, but now we can finally dive into them with greater detail. So without further ado, they are *omnipotent, omnipresent,* and *omniscient.*

Let's start with omnipotent: om·nip·o·tent [om níppətənt]. Omnipotent means "all-powerful: possessing complete, unlimited, or universal power and authority." It also implies sovereignty.

The term is used in Revelation 19:6, where it stands in for the Greek word "pantokrator". In total, "pantokrator" is used only ten times in the New Testament. In nine of those incidences, it is translated as Almighty. Eight of those are in Revelation, and elsewhere in Revelation it is translated as Omnipotent.

The Old Testament equivalent of this is Shadday, which is also translated as Almighty. There are forty-eight mentions of Almighty in the Old Testament. Almighty, or Shadday, indicates the fullness of God's grace. It would remind the Hebrew reader that from God comes every good and perfect gift, that He is never weary of pouring forth His mercies on His people, and that He is more ready to give than they are to receive.[3] This is the root of where we get the name of God, El Shadday. El (meaning God) and Shadday (meaning inexhaustible bounty). Our Lord is the God of inexhaustible bounty!

> Our Lord is the God of inexhaustible bounty!

And Jesus spoke unto them, saying, all power is given unto me in heaven and in earth (Matthew 28:18). The Greek word used here is "exousia", or authority. The idea being expressed is the right to exercise authority. In Matthew 10:1, we see that Jesus gave "exousia" to His disciples over the demonic realm before He went to the cross. This has to mean that Jesus never lost that dimension of authority; He only lost temporary rule over the earthly domain that Adam lost in the garden. He came to regain "exousia" over the earth and put it back in the hands of men.

In Luke 4:6, we see that Satan offers "exousia" to Jesus over the kingdoms of the world. This is what Adam lost. Satan usurped Adam's authority and was now offering it to Jesus. This also means that Satan had to actually posses this authority and be able to give it to Jesus, otherwise this would not have been a temptation. Satan said, *"That is delivered unto me; and to whomsoever I will I give it."* Notice that Jesus didn't question His authority in the matter, He just said, *"Thou shalt worship the Lord thy God and him only shalt thou serve"* (Luke 4:8).

Our next omni in the lineup is Omnipresent: om·ni·pres·ent [òmnee prézz'nt]. This word has two meanings. First, it means "always present everywhere: continuously and simultaneously present throughout the whole of creation." Another definition is "found everywhere: present or seemingly present all the time or everywhere."

Though we do not have a scripture with the word omnipresent directly stated, we have many allusions to it. In Matthew 28:20, Jesus says that *"I am with you always."* However, in John 16:7 we see that Jesus must leave for our best interest. *Nevertheless I tell you the truth; It is expedient for you that I go away: for if I go not away, the Comforter will not come unto you; but if I depart, I will send him unto you.*

Then, John 14:16, we see Jesus' prayer, *And I will pray the Father, and he shall give you another Comforter, that he may abide with you for ever."* It is an implied understanding here that the Holy Spirit will be with each believer who receives Him. One can postulate from this that He would have to be omnipresent in order to do so. The Holy Spirit is always present throughout the world. He is with believers and He draws the unbelievers to Jesus. He will never leave us or forsake us.

The last of our Omni's is omniscient: om·nis·cient [om níssee ənt]. Omniscient means "all-knowing: knowing or seeming to know everything."

We have several scripture references to look at revolving around the omniscience of God. I like to say that when God asks you a question, He isn't looking for information. He is giving you an opportunity. After Adam and Eve fell and God asked where they were, it wasn't because He didn't know. He was giving them the opportunity to come clean about disobeying His commandment. He was giving Adam a moment to contemplate the state he was in. He wanted Adam to realize the state he was in.

When Cain murdered Abel, God asked him where his brother was, giving him the same opportunity to realize what he had become and repent. Instead, Cain became defensive and asked, "Am I my brother's keeper?" God already knew that Abel was dead. There are numerous accounts like the ones I have just mentioned. When God asks you a question, stop and think before you answer. Chances are it's a rhetorical question. If He truly is looking for an answer, it is for your benefit, not His.

When God asks you a question, stop and think before you answer. Chances are it's a rhetorical question.

The first scripture I would like to look at is in Matthew. *And Jesus knowing their thoughts said, Wherefore think ye evil in your hearts?* (Matthew 9:4). Jesus knew what they were thinking, not by telepathy but by the condition of their heart. It is not the mind that really matters. It is the heart.

What follows is a rather lengthy passage, but it's loaded with pertinent information to many of the things we have talked about so far in the book.

But when the Pharisees heard it, they said, This fellow doth not cast out devils, but by Beelzebub the prince of the devils. And Jesus knew their thoughts, and said unto them, Every kingdom divided against itself is brought to desolation; and every city or house divided against itself shall not stand: and if Satan cast out Satan, he is divided against himself; how shall then his kingdom stand? And if I by Beelzebub cast out devils, by whom do your children cast them out? therefore they shall be your judges. But if I cast out devils by the Spirit of God, then the kingdom of God is come unto you. Or else how can one enter into a strong man's house, and spoil his goods, except he first bind the strong man? and then he will spoil his house. He that is not with me is against me; and he that gathereth not with me scattereth abroad. Wherefore I say unto you, All manner of sin and blasphemy shall be forgiven unto men: but the blasphemy against the Holy Ghost shall not be forgiven unto men. And whosoever speaketh a word against the Son of man, it shall be forgiven him: but whosoever speaketh against the Holy Ghost, it shall not be forgiven him, neither in this world, neither in the world to come. Either make the tree good, and his fruit good; or else make the tree corrupt, and his fruit corrupt: for the tree is known by his fruit. O generation of vipers, how can ye, being evil, speak good things? for out of the abundance of the heart the mouth speaketh. A good man out of the good treasure of the heart bringeth forth good things: and an evil man out of the evil treasure bringeth forth evil things. But I say unto you, That every idle word that men shall speak, they shall give account thereof in the day of judgment. For by thy words thou shalt be justified, and by thy words thou shalt be condemned (Matthew 12:24-37).

There's a lot of information in this passage. The first thing I want to look at in this passage is that, *They said, This fellow doth not cast out devils, but by Beelzebub the prince of the devils. And Jesus knew their thoughts, and said unto them...* If you look at this carefully, you see that "they said", but you also notice that Jesus "knew their thoughts". If Jesus knew their thoughts but they said something, apparently their heart was doing the talking, not their lips.

We see later in that passage, *for out of the abundance of the heart the mouth speaketh. A good man out of the good treasure of the heart bringeth forth good things: and an evil man out of the evil treasure bringeth forth evil things.* I talked more about this in my last book, *Entering Into The Hall of Faith*, for those who are interested.

The next thing we see in this passage is the infamous "a house divided" passage. I wish I could stress strongly enough just how critical this passage is. It is imperative that we grasp this concept that a house divided cannot stand. Another scripture that comes to mind here is Matthew 6:24: *No man can serve two masters: for either he will hate the one, and love the other; or else he will hold to the one, and despise the other. Ye cannot serve God and mammon.*

A divided house has two masters and will ultimately fall. It cannot stand. The Christians that I have seen make it are the ones that turn their back on the world and submerse themselves in the things of God. Their friends change, their music changes, their whole lifestyle changes, because they have been down the other road and know where it leads. They have found a better way to live and have run wholeheartedly toward God. These are few and far between but they do come along. Of course, this should come as no surprise. Jesus told us this. *Because strait is the gate, and narrow is the way, which leadeth unto life, and few there be that find it* (Matthew 7:14).

> **When you come to God, you forsake the old lifestyle and be faithful to your new Master.**

The best example I can think of to illustrate serving two masters would be marriage. When you get married, you stop seeing other people. You can't serve a wife and a girlfriend – at least not for very long. I would wake up dead, because my wife would kill me. Most people that start seeing someone else end up leaving their spouse and despising them, when truth be told they were the ones that cheated! If you were a player before you got married, you can't continue that lifestyle and stay married. If you love your wife, you give up all the other girls and are loyal and faithful to her alone. When you come to God, you forsake the old lifestyle and be faithful to your new Master. *Therefore shall a man leave his father and his mother, and shall cleave unto his wife: and they shall be one flesh* (Genesis 2:24). Keep this verse firmly in mind.

Jesus told the Pharisees, *Ye are of your father the devil, and the lusts of your father ye will do. He was a murderer from the beginning, and abode not in the truth, because there is no truth in him* (John 8:44). Before you were saved by God's grace through faith, your father was the devil. I know that may not fit with everyone's philosophy, but that doesn't change the fact that it is the truth.

There are only two masters: God and the devil. You either serve God by choice, or you serve the devil by default. There is no middle ground. When you come to God and accept Him as Lord and Savior, you need not serve the devil any longer. Don't ride the fence, jump it like a sprint runner over a hurdle and never look back! You can't serve two masters. God said He set before us life and death, blessing and cursing. You decide.

I managed to stray a little off course there, but I feel strongly about this. Let's look at the remainder of the passage from Matthew 12. *But I say unto you, That every idle word that men shall speak, they shall give account thereof in the day of judgment. For by thy words thou shalt be justified, and by thy words thou shalt be condemned.* We talked earlier in the book about sound waves being a form of energy and our words carrying weight. That is a heavy scripture when you consider that you will be judged for every word you speak. Our words are more important than we realize!

Let's look back at the omniscience of God. To do so, let's turn to 1 Corinthians. *For what man knoweth the things of a man, save the spirit of man which is in him? even so the things of God knoweth no man, but the Spirit of God* (1 Corinthians 2:11). In other words, a monkey doesn't know what it is like to be a man. Only a man does. I know the evolutionists think otherwise, but they are confounded in their own wisdom. Man cannot possibly know the things of God unless the Spirit of God reveals them to him. God, on the other hand, knows what it is like to be a man.

Seeing then that we have a great high priest, that is passed into the heavens, Jesus the Son of God, let us hold fast our profession. For we have not an high priest which cannot be touched with the feeling of our infirmities; but was in all points tempted like as we are, yet without sin. Let us therefore come boldly unto the throne of grace, that we may obtain mercy, and find grace to help in time of need (Hebrews 4:14-16).

We can't honestly say that God doesn't understand what we are going through, because He does. He's been there, done that, and has the scars to prove it! He walked the earth as a man and was tempted and tried in every way. He knows what it means to be a man in this realm.

Our next two scriptures tell of the same account, but do so from the perspective of two different Gospels. *But of that day and that hour knoweth no man, no, not the angels which are in heaven, neither the Son, but the Father* (Mark 13:32). *But of that day and hour knoweth no man, no, not the angels of heaven, but my Father only* (Matthew 24:36). We see here that some things only the Father knows. We saw earlier that God the Father had to reveal to Jesus the Son the Revelation that He is (in Revelation 1:1)

This brings me to a conjecture. We know that God is all at once omnipresent, omnipotent, and omniscient. Or all-knowing, all-powerful, and everywhere at once. We also know, but still don't truly understand, that God is One but also Three. This means that God is in a state of superposition Himself. Could it be that each of the Trinity contains only one aspect of the omnis but that together as God they contain all the aspects? Is this outside the realm of possibility?

We know His Spirit is in all the earth. Therefore, the Spirit would be omnipresent. We know that the Father is all-knowing and reveals things even to Jesus. That would make the Father omniscient. We also know that all power and authority has been given to Jesus after His resurrection. This would make Him omnipotent. Through entanglement, however, they could each take on the others' attributes instantly when needed, or when observed as necessary.

We also know that God is Light and that light is both a wave and a particle. When we observe it and try to catch the wave, so to speak, it becomes a particle. The two slit experiment doesn't work when we try to observe it. Could it be that the mystery is reserved so that we have to take some things on faith? We know that the wavelength of light is everywhere until we try to observe it, and only then does it become a particle – much like the Spirit of God. It is everywhere, but we can observe the Spirit at certain locations having specified effects at certain times. We know that the Spirit draws us to Jesus and that Jesus baptizes us into the Holy Spirit. For a word of wisdom or word of knowledge, or even in a prophetic utterance, the Holy Spirit would tap into the all-knowing side of the Father and draw out the information needed. If someone needs healing, the Holy Spirit would draw from the power and anointing of Jesus. The Father and Jesus would both be aware of everything happening in the earth through the observance of the Holy Spirit.

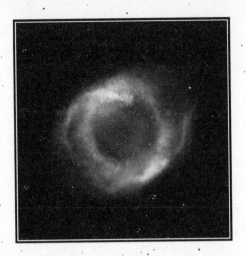

What Are the Odds?

Albert Einstein once said that "science without religion is lame, religion without science is blind."[6] What I hope I have managed to do with this book is open our blinded eyes to a new realm where science does not balk at scripture, but rather embraces it, where the two are not in direct opposition but are rather finely intertwined, where we can't throw the baby named Science out with the bath water of Religion because we don't agree with the temperature of the facts.

I believe that God could have very well created everything we see, and don't see, with a big bang. The concept that first there was nothing and then it exploded may very well prove to be true. It is possible that God spoke and that His

To believe that there was nothing, and nothing caused it to explode... is borderline dementia.

faith-filled words exploded and began creating the world as we know it. But to believe that there was nothing, and nothing caused it to explode, and then out of the nothingness evolved what we see today, is borderline dementia.

According to Occam's razor, "All other things being equal, the simplest solution is the best." They say Christians are crazy for believing in God and creation, but it takes far more faith to believe the universe happened on its own accord than it does to believe in God.

In physics, the odds of something happening by chance is defined as statistical probability. There are odds or statistics of an event occurring randomly. The probability of anything $<10^{50}$ is considered absurd. To explain, the odds of something happening by random chance being absurd is 1 in 100000000000000000000000000000000000000000000000000. I'm not even sure they have names for numbers that high. Those are pretty long odds, to say the least. The odds in winning the lottery where you have to choose six correct numbers between 1 and 54 are 1 in 25,827,165. Not absurd, but still something of a long shot.

Here are a couple of other interesting facts. You have a twelve times greater chance of being hit by lightning than winning the lottery. If you were a pregnant woman, you would have a three times greater possibility of giving birth to quadruplets than winning the lottery! These odds I have mentioned are rare. Very rare. Yet, our evolutionist friends would have us believe odds that life happened by chance when, with all of our knowledge and technology, we can't even reproduce those results in a lab! The odds of evolution occurring are 1 in infinity! It can't be done.

If people really believe in evolution, they should quit going to the doctor, because evolution is trying to evolve beyond them and flush the weak and sick out of the system. If they really believe evolution, then we shouldn't be trying to save the whales or the spotted owl, since evolution has apparently chosen those species to die off. To intervene would be equal to trying to stop the evolutionary process. The **only** way any of this came to be is by intelligent design.

Let's look at some specific odds for just a minute. In Joao Magueijo's book *Faster Than The Speed Of Light*, he describes how Robert Dicke described the flatness problem. Dicke, while giving a lecture at Cornell, wowed his audience by inserting numbers into the flatness problem. The flatness problem arises from the fact that gravitational energy had to delicately balance the cosmic energy of expansion without deviating from the constant value of Omega (or 1) during the big bang. It's okay if you don't follow the science here, so long as you follow my point. Dicke "showed that when the universe was one second old, the value of Omega must have been somewhere between 0.99999999999999999 and 1.00000000000000001. If Omega had deviated from one by more than this, either crunching or emptiness would have destroyed the universe a long time ago."[7]

However, if you go back to the shortest amount of measurable time after the universe started and measured, your odds skyrocket! If you go back to Planck time, which is 0.00000000000000000000 00000000000000000001 of a second, after the universe exploded, the odds of gravity and expansion dancing the line of Omega are absurd by their own standards! Omega had to be observed to between 0.999(followed by sixty more 9's) and 1.000(followed by sixty more 0's and then a 1). That's way beyond the absurd in random chance.

Even the big bang theory implies a designer had to be at the controls to keep Omega in check long enough for the universe to form. The odds of the universe

> Even the big bang theory implies a designer had to be at the controls.

coming from a big bang without a creator would be like a ballerina, in her point shoes, dancing, leaping, and twirling along a piece of fishing line (Omega) suspended from the center of the cosmos to the outer realms of the universe for the last fifteen billion years without falling or taking a break. Needless to say, those are pretty long odds.

Now let's look at something a little more concrete, something with less conjecture, something a little more relevant. Let's look at hemoglobin. Hemoglobin carries oxygen from the lungs, or gills (if you happen to be a fish), throughout the rest of the body. The hemoglobin molecule is made up of five hundred and seventy-four elements from an alphabet of twenty amino acids. These five hundred and seventy-four amino acids have to be strung together in just one of the possible combinations to form hemoglobin. The odds of these five hundred and seventy-four amino acids coming together by random chance in just the right order is 10^{650}! That's 1 in 1, followed by 650 zeros! Talk about absurd long shots.

That's just one aspect of our body. Other aspects are just as complex, and some even more so. Consider our DNA for a moment. Our DNA is a 3 out of 4, error-correcting, self-replicating code that consists of over **3 billion** elements defining the manufacture and arrangement of hundreds of thousands of devices, each device consisting of unique assemblies selected from over 200 proteins, each protein involving 3000 atoms in 3-dimensional configurations, all defined from an alphabet of 20 amino acids![8]

> The very concept of evolution breaks our own laws of physics.

The very concept of evolution breaks our own laws of physics. Anyone ever hear of the laws of thermodynamics? The law of conservation states that matter and energy can neither be created nor destroyed. Energy can only be changed from one form to another. The idea is that there is only a fixed amount of matter and energy in the universe, and that there can never be any more or any less, is a well-established scientific fact. This is the first law in thermodynamics.

The second law of thermodynamics is the law of entropy. The basis of the law of entropy is that, given time, through a process, all things will reach an equilibrium. For example, if I set a hot cup of coffee on my desk and a cold glass of water beside it, given time they will both reach the ambient temperature of the room. It is through entropy that we say the coffee got cold and the water got hot, although they have actually reached the same temperature.

Things tend to devolve from order to chaos. If you don't believe me, look at the world around you. We constantly have to build jails. There are more murders now than there have ever been. There is more lawlessness than there has ever been. That's what you get when you take God out of the classroom and teach that we came from a bowl of biotic soup, that there is no God, and that there is nothing beyond this life. If this is all there is, then there are no consequences. If there are no consequences, then self-preservation kicks into overdrive and lawlessness prevails. The human race is evolving, but it's in reverse order … from the perfection of the Garden of Eden into the chaos we live in today.

I once heard a creationist discussing a debate he once had at a university with a group of professors who teach evolution. As he talked about Noah taking only two dogs on the ark, a master breed so to speak, and that all breeds we have today come from those two dogs, the professors began to scoff. Their ridiculing question was, "You expect us to believe that over four hundred breeds of dogs came from just two dogs?" To this, he replied, "Yet you expect me to believe that the same four hundred breeds of dogs came from a pile of goo." That is the tainted biased logic these people have. They scoff at things that are rational, and yet believe something that is beyond the realm of reason and defies all logic.

True science is supposed to be unbiased with an open view, but being the humans we are, we all tend to go into things with a preconceived notion. While I do certainly believe in the bible and its infallibility, I try to stay within the realm of being objective. I don't want to just slap something together and call it science that proves the existence of God. I want to look at all the facts openly and make a well-informed decision. I don't want to overstate information in a zealous effort to prove the Truth, nor do I want to try and water down and dilute the Truth to fit my own ideas. At the same time, a good bit of this book is conjecture based on personal revelation. It is what I feel the Holy Spirit has led me to write concerning the issues as we looked at them.

On the opposite side of the debate, everything that they want to teach about evolution at our public schools is also mere conjecture. However, a great deal of their conjecture can be easily rebutted or discredited. But you never hear about that, do you? No. Instead it is presented as fact while they mock a much more plausible and scientifically reliable conjecture based on intelligent design.

These subjects have been a great deal of fun to research while I wrote this book. These subjects are left to conjecture, in my opinion, because they are not the endgame. While these matters are interesting and fun to read about, they are not as important as our salvation. You can judge the importance of the topic in the bible by the amount of text devoted to it. We have a limited creation account because it is not that large a piece of the puzzle. Creation is important in that it forms the rest of your theology.

There are really only two kinds of creation beliefs. Either you believe in a higher power and an intelligent design of the universe, or you believe in evolution and that there is nothing beyond this life. I hope that I have presented you with some new, thought-provoking ideas. I hope you have enjoyed the journey you've taken with me.

May God bless you and keep you. May His grace, mercy, and favor shine upon you. Until next time, whatever that subject may be, all blessing, honor, power, and praise belong to my Lord and Savior Jesus Christ. Amen.

Bibliography

1 *E=Einstein: His Life, His Thought, and His Influence on Our Culture*, published by Sterling Publishing Co., Inc © 2006 Article by Brian Greene

2 *The Science of God* by Gerald L. Schroeder,

3 Strong's Concordance

4 E. Schrodinger, Proceedings of the Cambridge Philosophical Society, 31 (1935), 555.

5 John Archibald Wheeler, "Law Without Law", Wheeler and Zureck eds., pg 182-3

6 *Science, Philosphy, and Religion: a Symposium* 1941

7 *Faster Than The Speed Of Light: The Story Of A Scientific Speculation*, by Joao Magueijo New York, Ny: Penguin Group, 2003 (ISBN 0-385-48499-2)

8 *The Book of Genesis*, by Chuck Missler – supplemental notes © 2004 Koinonia House Inc. (I highly recommend this comprehensive study of Genesis, a study from which I have learned a great deal. I relied heavily on it throughout my research for this book. It is the most thorough and complete study of Genesis I have found.

9 *Commentary on Genesis*, Nachmonides 1263

I also recommend David Van Koevering's book "Elsewhen" and all of his materials. This can be obtained on his website at www.elsewhen.com. While I did not directly quote from his work, he has had a great impact on my life and I did reference him several times throughout the text. His work is very thought-provoking in the area of science and the bible. I thank you David for all the input you have had in my life, knowingly and unknowingly.

About the Author

Bobby Lynn resides in Huntsville, Alabama. He has been married for 18 years to his wonderful wife Tammy. They have two children Tyler and Madison.

He was an associate Pastor until God recently lead him to resign and pursue writing. He has traveled to South Africa where he has ministered to leaders and their congregations. He still supports and is contact with five churches in South Africa.

His passion is to teach God's people to walk in the fullness of God and see God's people rise up and fulfill their destiny in the Kingdom. He can be reached at bobby@theeternalnow.com.

Visit my website at www.theeternalnow.com.

Also Available by **Bobby Lynn...**

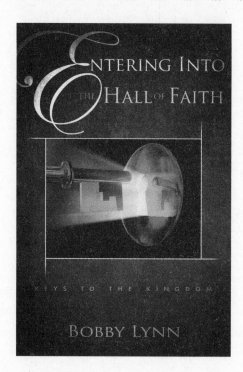

ENTERING THE HALL OF FAITH
Keys to the Kingdom

BOBBY LYNN

ISBN: 978-0-924748-86-8
UPC: 88571300056-7
6x9 Trade Paper
Retail: $14.99

*A*s you're about to find out for yourself, Hall of Faith is full of insightful and relevant nuggets of truth that have the ability to change your life forever. You could mine its pages for days on end without using it up. With strength and vision, author Bobby Lynn takes you on a thought-provoking journey through the Christian experience, weaving a clear avenue for faith-filled living.

The knowledge in these pages are things that are not commonly known or understood, but need to be. With the guidance contained in this book, you can finally take the ultimate step of entering the Hall of Faith. This is what you've been waiting your whole life for.

PERSONAL NOTES

_____

_____

_____

_____

_____

_____

_____

_____

_____

_____

_____

_____

_____

_____

_____